# The Shepherd's Rod
# 2020

## By Bonnie Jones and Lyn Kost

White Horses Publishing
Pineville, North Carolina

# The Shepherd's Rod 2020:
## Copyright © 2019 by Bonnie Jones and Lyn Kost

Printed in the United States of America.

Cover art created by Lyn Kost (704)-975-9631 lyn@bobjones.org

To obtain more of Bob and Bonnie Jones' written, video and audio teachings, prophecies and materials visit us at www.DidYouLearnToLove.org

or write to: White Horses Publishing
P.O. Box 838
Pineville, N.C. 28134-0838

# Introduction to
# The Shepherd's Rod

The Day of Atonement (Yom Kippur) is signified in Scripture as one of the most important dates of the Biblical year since the time of Moses. This sacred day continues as a most significant Holy Day even in the present Church age.

For many years Bob Jones has received valuable revelations on this day outlining activities of the Holy Spirit for the seasons ahead. These insights have historically proven to be accurate and strategic blueprints for spiritual emphasis and preparation.

The term "Shepherd's Rod" derives its meaning from *Ezekiel 20:37* stating:

> And I shall make you pass under the rod and I shall bring you into the bond of the covenant. *(Ezekiel 20:37)*

This Scripture symbolically portrays a shepherd extending his rod as his sheep pass under the staff for evaluation. In like manner, we as the Lord's sheep, pass under His staff during this season for the same purpose. *Jeremiah 33:13* and *Leviticus 27:32* provide more clarity in this Biblical principle.

# TABLE OF CONTENTS

Chapters 1 – 5 by Bonnie Jones
Chapters 6 – 8   by Lyn Kost

# Forward

Transition, patience, sounding the alarm and the belt of truth are just part of this year's prophetic forecast. As the body of Christ transitions from seeing the word to declaring it, you will observe increased levels of anointed prophetic words released through surrendered vessels. The body of Christ has been crossing the Jordon for a period of time now. Many Christians focus was only on getting their feet wet, while many others were totally submerged and have already crossed to the other side. I believe this is the remnant and they are now beckoning the lingerers to come join them.

Moses and Aaron were anointed to take the Israelites to the edge of the Jordan River. The Promised Land lay on the other side. Unfortunately these two mighty men of God were not permitted to enter the Promised Land. Why? Did God have a last minute decision to make because His two friends disobeyed? (Numbers 20:12) Of course not! Their anointing took them only as far as it could and no further. It was time for Israel's next leaders to step up and take the reins. They would take the new generation into the land flowing with milk and honey. And the same is true today. There are well trained and equipped replacements on the horizon that must come forth.

The body has been parked at the river's bank long enough. It's time for a new circumcision but it's not of the flesh. This time it's a circumcision of our hearing and thoughts. God wants to bring our hearing as well as our thoughts into covenant with Him. (Jeremiah 6:10) Then behold what we speak with our mouth will be a declaration that moves heaven and shakes the earth. Now is the time to cross over the Jordan and blow the trumpet. As it was with Jericho, so shall it be with our enemies. And the walls of resistance shall come down. (Joshua 6:20)

In each generation the body of Christ dealt with patience. And it has learned many critical lessons throughout scripture and the importance of patient endurance. Job, Noah, Moses and Joseph are just a few of our heroes that patiently endured tough times. Bob Jones definition of patience is "enduring life without complaint!" And that pretty well wraps it up. However most of us fail in that department daily. But we have our forefathers that set powerful examples. And if you study each one you will understand the rewards patient endurance afforded them. The writer of Hebrews said it best regarding our Lord Jesus, the author and finisher of our faith, "who for the joy that was set before Him endured the cross, despising the shame, and has sat down at the right hand of the throne of God." (Hebrews 12:2)

Over the years the body of Christ has matured on different levels overcoming many of the enemy's schemes. One of the most important areas Christians have matured in is the bridling of the tongue. (James 2:2-10) Perhaps it's the most difficult because it goes hand in hand with impatience. Out of the fullness of our heart the mouth speaks. (Matthew 12:34b) So if we are angry, bitter, resentful or impatient we speak from that vantage point. Therefore until we can patiently endure each circumstance we tend to grumble and complain like the children of Israel. Their complaining caused the whole first generation to not enter the Promised Land.

This is the year and decade of the mouth. Therefore I believe mature saints are going to declare the revelation they receive. They will speak in agreement with the Holy Spirit and it shall be established. The Lord declared the mouth to be a horn, bugle and trumpet to sound the alarm during this time of the greatest harvest the earth has ever known. Death and life are in the power of the tongue, and those who love it will eat its fruit (Proverbs 18:21) Get ready to see miracles in the midst as Christians with bridled tongues speak in agreement with the Holy Spirit and demonstrate resurrection life. There is no more delay and what they speak "shall be on earth as it is in heaven." (Matthew 6:10)

The body of Christ can no longer take things for granted because the Lord is tightening His belt of truth around His children. (Ephesians 6:14) They are called to greater levels of intimacy with the Holy Spirit and accountability to the Father. Then when the devil comes knocking at the door of their soul they will not fall into temptation because they are girded with His Truth. Therefore they will walk in truth and love. Because love measures truth and truth measures love.

So get ready for an exciting year as the body of Christ crosses their personal Jordan with a clear trumpet call declaring the word in truth. Watch for anointed leaders to come to the forefront and lead the body into new spiritual realms. Transition is inevitable so don't fight it, move with it. Don't just get your feet wet. Cross to the other side and receive the blessings of yes and amen reserved for this generation.

# THE SHEPHERD'S ROD
## 2020

# Chapter One
## Year of the Mouth
## 2020 or 5780

The last decade 5770-5779 (from 2010 to 2019) has been all about "seeing." "Ayin" is the 16th letter of the Hebrew alphabet whose picture symbol is an eye and its numerical value is the number 70. The "eye" is to see, understand and obey. Jeremiah 5:21 says, *"Hear now this, O foolish people without understanding or heart, who have eyes and see not, who have ears and hear not."* Ayin can also be a silent letter therefore representing humility because it sees but does not speak. This also indicates wisdom and discernment. DON'T CAST PEARLS

## The Decade to Declare

This year, beginning with Rosh Hashanah, it's all about speaking or declaring. This decade 5780-5789 (from 2020 to 2029) is the Hebrew letter "Pey." It is the 17th letter of the Hebrew alphabet whose picture symbol is a mouth. And its' numerical value is the number 80. The mouth represents speech, power and communication. And the number 80 represents spiritual strength. Therefore I believe that in this decade we will declare with our mouth what the eye has seen in the last decade.

For the past decade our focus has been on seeing into the heavenly realm and gaining greater spiritual revelation. Many of the spiritual truths the Lord showed the body of believers is for a future date. By this I mean, He's been carefully grooming His bride and watching over her as she matures. The Lord told Jeremiah that He was watching over His word to perform it. (Jeremiah 1:12) After all it's His word that His children will declare by the Spirit of Truth. God's words have creative power when spoken through pure vessels. He will perform the very action they decree because He has spoken it into their spirit forming a unity with Him. Then it becomes on earth as it is in heaven.

*Then said the Lord to me, you have seen well, for I am alert and active, watching over My word to perform it. (Jeremiah 1:12)*

In this past decade the body of Christ received plenty of revelation yet was not permitted to share some of it. It's been a matter of trust and obedience because they go hand in hand. She's also had to learn the difficult yet vital lesson of bridling her tongue. (James 1:26) Loose lips sink ships but wisdom and discernment will keep the ship afloat.

*If anyone thinks himself to be religious (piously observant of the external duties of his faith) and does not bridle his tongue but deludes his own heart, this person's religious service is worthless (futile, barren). (James 1:26)*

The mature bride has endured character assassination yet spoke not a word. Instead she allowed the Lord to fight her battles.

She had to bridle her tongue while keeping her eyes on the Lord. In Exodus 14 when the Israelite children stood at the mouth of the Red Sea with Pharaoh's army bearing down on them, Moses told the people, *"Fear not; stand still (firm, confident, undismayed) and see the salvation of the Lord which He will work for you today. For the Egyptians you have seen today you shall never see again. The Lord will fight for you, and you shall hold your peace and remain at rest.*

In the past decade the body of Christ learned greater humility and how to bridle the tongue. All of this was preparation for this decade so she can now speak forth the oracles of God. She is not speaking from her soul. No, she is speaking from a sanctified mind in agreement with her spirit empowered by the Holy Spirit. And when she opens her mouth God will fill it.

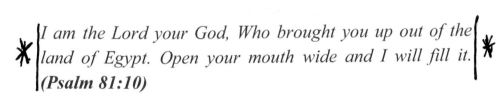

*I am the Lord your God, Who brought you up out of the land of Egypt. Open your mouth wide and I will fill it.*
***(Psalm 81:10)***

## Hung By Their Tongue

The Lord reminded me of a vision He gave me on the Day of Atonement several years ago. Here is a partial excerpt from the 2017 Shepherd's Rod.

As I peered into this vision I could see a long narrow hallway where there appeared to be two stonewalls opposite each other. Securely notched into the stone were silver metal eyehooks spaced evenly apart and about five or six feet off the floor. Attached to the each eyehook was a hangman's noose with only a short amount of rope. People literally had their necks against the wall. It was obvious they were given just enough rope to hang themselves. This was very strange but people were hanging there until they were dead. It was obvious their lies had caught up to them. They had gone passed the point of return.

## Three Biblical Examples

Then the Lord showed me biblical characters that were literally hung by their tongue. Ananias lied to the Holy Spirit about the amount of the sale of his property and God killed him. And only a few hours later when Peter confronted his wife Sapphira, she lied also. Sapphira was unaware of her husband's demise. And God killed her also. Peter said that Satan filled their heart to lie to the Holy Spirit. **(Acts 5:3, 4b&5)** Because of their hypocrisy and deceit, God struck them dead. **(Acts 5:7-9)**

Haman was given just enough rope to hang himself. Thinking he was building a gallows for Mordecai, he in fact built it for himself. Haman was literally hung by his own tongue when all of his evil plots and schemes were exposed. **(Esther 7:5-6)**

Judas Iscariot plotted against the Lord. He went to the chief priest and betrayed Jesus for thirty pieces of silver. **(Matthew 26:14-16)** Through his words Judas plotted this evil scheme that started the wheel in motion to crucify Christ. Once he shared his plan with the priests the ball was set in motion and it was too late to turn back.

In each of these stories you see the main character hatching a scheme of evil intent. In one way or another, the devil entered into them through a form of pride. For the love of money Ananias, Sapphria and Judas would lie to the Holy Spirit and betray Christ. And Haman's pride was self-prominence. He was going to be the big man on the block that destroyed the Jews.

Man can run, hide, lie, cheat and steal but he can never escape an all knowing God. He keeps an account of all things and will give man just enough rope to hang himself through his own lying schemes. But His mercy is always available if man will only repent. All mankind is accountable for their words and actions. And in the end God's justice shall prevail.

*Then those who feared the Lord spoke to one another, and the Lord listened and heard them; so a book of remembrance was written before Him For those who fear the Lord and who meditate on His name. (Malachi 3:16)*

## The Spoken Word

In 2010 the Lord spoke to me, "You must take an aggressive ✳ stand against the spoken word because it gives the enemy permission to use them against you. You must cancel the power and authority against the spoken word!" The only power the enemy has is through our words. As He spoke this to me I saw a

EVERY TONGUE RISES IN JUDGEMENT

large whirlwind with word curses like depression, anxiety, hatred, anger, fear, lies, immorality and infirmity. They were swirling out of control and being hurled toward the earth.

That's why it's vital that we bridle our tongue. When we speak out of anger, jealousy, hatred or fear we're agreeing with the plan of the enemy. Many things we speak have a twist to it. They have self-centered motives. In Psalm 19 the psalmist say, *"Let the words of my mouth and the meditation of my heart be acceptable in Your sight, O Lord, my strength and my Redeemer."* We speak out of the fullness of our heart **(Luke 6:45)** so whatever sits on the throne of our soul will flow out of our mouth. And once the negative word is out in the air, the enemy has full court advantage. Remember, the devil is the prince of the power of the air. **(Ephesians 2:2)**

*A good man out of the good treasure of his heart brings forth good; and an evil man out of the evil treasure of his heart brings forth evil. For out of the abundance of the heart his mouth speaks.* **(Luke 6:45 NKJV)**

## Enemy's Access

*For My thoughts are not your thoughts, neither are your ways My ways, says the Lord. For as the heavens are higher than the earth, so are My ways higher than your ways and My thoughts than your thoughts.* **(Isaiah 55:8-9)**

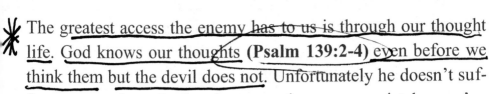

The greatest access the enemy has to us is through our thought life. God knows our thoughts **(Psalm 139:2-4)** even before we think them but the devil does not. Unfortunately he doesn't suffer memory loss. In fact he remembers every mistake you've made, every stronghold you've overcome and every sin that's been forgiven. And he will use these things against you with each opportunity you give him. Satan knows you've made great strides as a spirit filled believer, but if he can prompt you to start down a bunny trail in your thought process, he wins. Because one wrong thought will lead to the second and so on until you begin verbalizing that first thought. And without our thoughts being brought under control, they turn into unforgiving words that spew out of Satan's whirlwind.

*You know my down sitting and my uprising; you understand my thoughts afar off. You sift and search out my path and my lying down, and you are acquainted with all my ways. For there is not a word on my tongue [still unuttered], but, behold, O Lord, You know it altogether.* **(Psalm 139:2-4)**

## Taking Thoughts Captive

In 2 Corinthians 10:5, Paul tells us to take every thought captive and bring them into the obedience of Christ. I believe this is exactly what believers must do. The enemy is relentless and continues prodding our thoughts. Years ago I prayed and asked God to not allow any of my thoughts turn into words that I would speak and harm someone. That one prayer radically transformed my ability to speak unkindly toward others. I literally thought before I spoke. Like my mother used to say, "If you can't say something nice about someone, don't speak at all!" And my saying is, "Don't say anything behind someone's back that you can't say to their face!" These two things keep me in check.

The prophet Jeremiah makes an astonishing statement. He declares that the ears of the people are not circumcised and never brought into covenant with God. We could say it's a cutting away of our carnal (fleshly) thoughts. The fact is we've never surrendered our hearing to the Lord. *To whom shall I [Jeremiah] speak and give warning that they may hear? Behold, their ears are uncircumcised [never brought into covenant with God or consecrated to His service], and they cannot hear or obey. Behold, the word of the Lord has become to them a reproach and the object of their scorn; they have no delight in it.* **(6:10)** If you're alive and breathing you continue to hear. Perhaps you have no choice in some of the things you hear. However you have a choice in receiving it into your spirit. After all, the hearing ear is the last organ to shut down in a natural death. Therefore you're hearing up until your last breath or heartbeat. That's why Paul tells us to bring every thought into captivity to the obedience of Christ. **(2 Corinthians 10:5b)** *For the weapons of our warfare are not carnal but mighty in God for pulling down strongholds, casting down arguments and every high thing that exalts itself against the knowledge of God.* **(2 Corinthians 10:4-5a)**

Jeremiah 6:10

Thoughts take action through our obedience to them. We are accountable for our thoughts as well as our words. Although the enemy doesn't know our thoughts he knows exactly the right buttons to push. And once we're off track we've come into agreement with him to release a curse through an unsanctified tongue. By doing so we have given our kingdom authority and power over to the enemy. Then the fruit of our thoughts demonstrated by our words are defiled and the enemy uses them against us for his gain. Jeremiah said that God brought evil upon the people due to the fruit of their thoughts. (Jeremiah 6:19)

*Hear, O earth: behold, I am bringing evil upon this people, the fruit of their thoughts (their schemes and devices) because they have not listened and obeyed My words, and as for My law, they have rejected it. **(Jeremiah 6:19)***

Let's take our thoughts captive and submit them to our spirit. Then surrender our spirit unto the Holy Spirit. By doing this we are more apt to think before we speak. And we will only speak words in love through obedience to the Lord. We will speak words of power to heal and words of encouragement to strengthen. And our words will be in alignment with God's heart of love for all mankind.

## No More Delay!

On the Day of Atonement I had a dream where I'm seated at a table on a second floor patio overlooking a semi-busy street. Across the street is a lovely park with playground, benches and a walking path. The grass and shrubs are well manicured while a variety of flowers paint a lovely backdrop. I'm told that, "When you pray you need to believe what you say and it shall be. There's no more delay! Just speak and it will be!" Then I looked across the street to the park. To my surprise a gentle flowing river had replaced the street. And people that would normally cross the street from the park simply walked through the river with ease. There was no hesitation, they just continued walking as if they're crossing the street. They weren't surprised; everyone just kept walking to get to the other side. They were dressed in business, casual and school clothes. I noticed that the water is up to everyone's waist. No matter how tall or short the individual, when they crossed the water reached their waist. According to Ezekiel 47 the waist represents commitment.

*Again he measured one thousand and brought me through; the water came up to my waist. (Ezekiel 47:4b NKJV)*

I believe this is a picture of Christians walking by faith and not by sight. We have not because we ask not and when we do ask, often times it's with wrong heart motives. And the Lord is saying that there is a body of committed believers who walk by faith that are now ready to cross their personal Jordan. And there's no more delay because they've died to self by aligning their heart with Him. Their motives are pure and not self-seeking because they have sought first the kingdom of God and His righteousness.

*But seek first the kingdom of God and His righteousness, and all these things shall be added to you. (**Matthew 6:33 NKJV**)*

## Ezekiel's River

I also feel that as these people enter this river they will bring others with them. Some will come for salvation; others for baptism while others will come for healing. Ezekiel 47 gives us a picture of waters that flow from under the threshold of the temple and Ezekiel is called to measure it four times. Each time it increases a thousand cubits. At first it was ankle-deep **(verse 3)** which means salvation and then knee-deep. The knee refers to prayer and intercession. **(Verse 4a)** Again he measured a thousand cubits and was caused to pass through the waters. And now the waters reached to his loins. **(Verse 4b)** The loins or waist indicates our commitment to Christ. And that's where I believe many in the body of Christ are today. They are totally committed to Christ and now ready to bring others into the waters for salvation, deeper relationship with Christ and healing. It's all part of the harvest and they are the harvesters.

We're not quite ready for verse 5. *Afterward he measured a thousand cubits, and it was a river that I could not pass through, for the waters had risen, waters to swim in, a river that could not be passed over or through.* I believe that when we actually swim in the river of God we will experience miracles, signs and wonders on a consistent basis. But in the meantime we are partakers of the crossing into and abiding in the river of God. It's a picture of dedicated Christians bringing others to the river of God for whatever their need may be.

The years the body spent learning to bridle its tongue have been well worth the wait. Spiritually mature Christians will now speak forth in confidence. Say what you mean and mean what you say and get ready to see your words take form. Job 22:28 says that you shall also decide and decree a thing, and it shall be established for you; and the light [of God's favor] shall shine upon your ways. So boldly speak what God gives you, nothing more and nothing less. Then when you decree a thing it will be established.

# Chapter Two
# Horn, Bugle, Trumpet!

A profound statement awakened me from a sound sleep as I heard the Lord saying;

**"The mouth is a horn, bugle and trumpet! Sound the alarm for My army to arise! Call them to order, says God! This is not a test. It's an order and a command from the Almighty on High."**

To bring better understanding of this incredible statement, I want to break it down into two different sections.

**First - "The mouth is a horn, bugle and trumpet! Sound the alarm for My army to arise! Call them to order, says God!**

The horn, bugle and trumpet are interchangeable in scripture. The word trumpet and horn are mentioned many times, however I found only one scripture referring to bugle and it's only in a few translations. In the midst of explaining the importance of speaking in tongues, Paul says, *"And if the war bugle gives an uncertain (indistinct) call, who will prepare for battle?" (1 Corinthians 14:8)* He is referring to tongues being unintelligible. In the same way a bugle makes a distinct sound yet it is very limited in its ability to perform. The bugle is a brass instrument like a small trumpet, typically without valves or keys. It is used for military signals such as reveille and taps. Therefore it cannot make the beautiful harmonious clear sound like the trumpet or horn. Paul goes on to say in verse 9, "*Just so it is with you; if you in the [unknown] tongue speak words that are not intelligible, how will anyone understand what you are saying? For you will be talking into empty space!*"

## Bugle Sounds Reveille

I believe the aforementioned scripture earmarks the difference. Tongues are to the believer like the bugle that gives a distinct sound or battle cry. But the mouth is like the trumpet or horn that proclaims the spoken word and advances the army of God. Now the Lord is saying, "Sound the alarm for My army to arise! So we must arouse the army of God by sounding Reveille.

In the United States Army the bugle is used to sound reveille. This signals the troops to awaken the soldiers for morning roll call. The raising of the flag thus representing the official beginning of the new day follows reveille. I believe this is a new day and the army of God is being called to arise and come to order.

*Blow the trumpet in Zion, and sound an alarm in My holy mountain! (Joel 2:1a)*

**Second - This is not a test! It's an order and a command from the Almighty on High."**

**This is not a test!** The body of Christ has been in a time of testing for a long time. And this was necessary in order to sift the wheat from the chaff and establish the nature of Christ in the body. It took forty years in the wilderness to bring forth a generation worthy of entering into the Promised Land. And so it is today. The sifting has taken place and now the body at large is ready to cross the Jordan.

**It's an <u>order and a command</u> from the Almighty on High.** El Shaddai, the all-powerful One has spoken. God spoke to Abram in Genesis 17:1 and told him to <u>walk before Him and be blameless.</u> I believe this is the command to the army of God in this day. We are called to walk in His likeness being holy and blameless. And to know Him as the Almighty God who will go before them in battle and deliver them from the snare of the fowler.

*UPRIGHTLY*

To command is to have authority over something or be in charge of it, such as an army. To order is to arrange or position something in place. I believe the command is being trumpeted now. And God's army is being called to order and divided into companies, battalions, and regiments. In the same way the children of Israel were divided into twelve tribes.

# Raise The Flag
## Take The Mountaintops

I was told to be the first to the mountaintop and place the flag. After reveille is played and the troops are awakened, immediately the flag is raised. It's vital in this day that Christians are the first to the mountaintop and raise God's victory flag. There can be no more delay. Once His army starts marching in formation, you will see the raising of the flag on all seven mountains; education, religion, family, business, government, entertainment and media. This is not a one-man show. It's going to take a company of men to accomplish this feat. It reminds me of the American flag being raised on Mount Suribachi, Iwo Jima. It took six marines in 1943 to secure the flag. Six is the number of man because man was created on the sixth day. And God said it was very good.

The Lord is giving His army instruction to carry forth His word. It's Joel's army arising and going forth because the Lord gives voice before His army, for His camp is very great; for strong is the One who executes His word. For the day of the Lord is great and very terrible; who can endure it? *(Joel 2:11)*

Now get ready to hear the sounding of the bugle playing taps as the enemy is defeated and God's banner rests atop the mighty mountains of the world's system. Joel 2:1a says, "Let all the inhabitants of the land tremble; for the day of the Lord is coming, for it is at hand."

# Resurrecting Old Ideas

Once again the Lord made another profound statement. Quickly I scribed this amazing account and prayed for understanding.

**Hear this says God; "I'm resurrecting old ideas of the past centuries, thoughts that I gave to others they never fulfilled. I have so many and they are countless. I've given to others in the past but fear kept them away from being successful in Me. Now today I'm financing My kingdom through My people with inventions that will launch a new society in Me."**

Then the Holy Spirit showed me a list of promises. However I was unable to remember them once I came out of this experience. I believe this list includes promises the Lord gave to prior generations that will be fulfilled in this generation and the ones yet to come. I believe there were many reasons that kept them from fulfilling those promises. Both faith and fear played a major role in the outcome.

Hebrews 11:1 says, now faith is the substance of things hoped for, the evidence of things not seen. And Proverbs 9:10 says, the fear of the Lord is the beginning of wisdom, and the knowledge of the Holy One is understanding. I prefer the amplified classic translation of Hebrews 11:1 because it refers to the substance as the "title deed." Therefore it means we already have ownership of the substance although we cannot see it.

I believe the Lord is saying that over the centuries He gave many Christians brilliant ideas but fear prevented them from bringing it into being. Fear of man, fear of failure and fear of the unknown gripped their heart. What if it doesn't work? How will I finance it? Is this really from God? These are just a few of the questions flooding their mind that caused them to lay the project aside. Eventually God's idea became a faded memory yet occasionally they pondered "what if?" Fear of failure was greater than the hope of God's promise. Fear cast a giant shadow that prevented the birthing of His ideas. I believe there were numerous inventions that never got off the ground because of low self-esteem. And many never got off the drawing pad.

But God has not forgotten His promises. He's been patiently waiting for a generation that will trust Him with all their heart and not lean on their own understanding. Because they acknowledge Him in all their ways, He shall direct their paths. *(Proverbs 3:5)* This generation has come to know their Master's voice and come boldly to His throne of grace. They walk in confidence knowing who they are in Christ and who He is in them. They boldly declare, *"The Lord is my helper; I will not fear. What can man do to me?" (Hebrews 13:6 NKJV)*

## Blueprints From Heaven

I believe we are going to see new inventions in science and technology as well as simple home improvements. Where previous generations laid aside God's plan, this generation is going to pick up the ball and run with it. Get ready for blueprints from heaven as He releases them to a body of believers who not only love God but also fear Him. Proverbs 15:33 says, *the fear of the Lord is the instruction of wisdom, and before honor is humility. (NKJV)*

God has given each generation opportunities to advance the kingdom yet most have failed. Many in the past that were successful used it for self-gain while others invested in an unwisely manner that supported the world system. Now get ready to see the transfer of wealth as God's children create His ideas. And when this happens, the world system will sow into and support kingdom ideas.

*A good man leaves an inheritance to his children's children, but the wealth of the sinner is stored up for the righteous. (Proverbs 13:22 NKJV)*

## Lord's New Society

I believe the Lord's new society will be comprised of totally dedicated Christians whose life reflects the nature of Christ. They are not looking for a get rich scheme to make them famous among men. No! Out of love for the Lord and obedience to the Father they follow a blueprint of heaven. They walk by faith and have no fear of man. God is the anchor of their hope and in Him all the promises are yes and amen.

I believe this new society is reserved for the seed of Abraham because they are the heirs of promise. And God cannot change!

When speaking to Abraham, He swore by Himself, saying, *"Surely blessing I will bless you, and multiplying I will multiply you." (Hebrews 6:14)* We're looking at the Melchizedek priesthood coming forth in love, honor, faith, truth, confidence and obedience. They live by faith not fear and display power from being in His presence. God has been waiting for a generation on whom He can bestow the promise He swore to Abraham.

*For when God made a promise to Abraham, because He could swear by no one greater, He swore by Himself, saying, "Surely blessing I will bless you, and multiplying I will multiply you." And so, after he had patiently endured, he obtained the promise. For men indeed swear by the greater, and an oath for confirmation is for them an end of all dispute. Thus God, determining to show more abundantly to the heirs of promise the immutability of His counsel, confirmed it by an oath, that by two immutable things, in which it is impossible for God to lie, we might have strong consolation, who have fled for refuge to lay hold of the hope set before us. This hope we have as an anchor of the soul, both sure and steadfast, and which enters the Presence behind the veil, where the forerunner has entered for us, even Jesus, having become High Priest forever according to the order of Melchizedek. (Hebrews 6:13-20 NKJV)*

I believe that in the time of the greatest harvest of souls God is blessing His children abundantly so they in turn can bless new believers. Remember this, many of the souls being harvested will be homeless people, junkies and prostitutes that will need housing and rehabilitation. Oh yes many will be business people, movie stars and people of prominence. Yet the great majority will be homeless and their lives will be radically transformed. And the true heirs of salvation, Abraham's seed, will welcome them with open arms. This is God's new society where brethren will dwell together in unity. *Behold, how good and how pleasant it is for brethren to dwell together in unity!* *(Psalm 133:1 NKJV)*

# Chapter Three
# Our Belt Of Truth Is Being Tightened

## The Belt of Truth

The belt of truth is the first piece of the "full armor of God" to be listed in Ephesians 6:10-17. The apostle Paul says to "be strong in the Lord and in the strength of His might." This is the key to understanding the armor of God. All the pieces of the armor belong to Him and come from Him. Truth, righteousness, the gospel, faith, and salvation—all are gifts of God to His people for their defense. All except "the sword of the Spirit, which is the Word of God" **(verse 17)** are defensive in nature. All are designed to help us "stand against the schemes of the devil" **(verse 11)**. The belt of truth is the first part of the armor listed because without truth we are lost and the schemes of the devil will surely overpower us.

I believe that the belt of truth is the first piece of armor listed because Jesus said that He is the Way, the Truth and the Life **(John 14:6)** and it is only through Him that we come to God. Therefore, truth is of the greatest importance in the life of a Christian. Without truth, the rest of the armor would be of no use to us because we would not have the Spirit of truth **(John 15:26)**.                INTEGRITY

In describing the whole armor of God, Paul gives us the image of a Roman soldier ready for battle. A soldier's belt was made

*1 Peter 1:13 Gird up the loins of your mind /*

of thick heavy leather and a metal band with a protective piece hanging down from the front of it. The belt held the soldier's sword as well as other weapons. The belt of truth for our spiritual armor holds the sword of the Spirit, linking truth and the Word of God because the Word of God is truth. **(John 17:17)**

Every Christian must take hold of the belt of truth and use it. It is a crucial piece of defensive armor guarding our innermost being in the battle against the lies and deceptions of the enemy. Without an understanding of truth, we are left defenseless and can easily be "tossed to and fro and carried about with every wind of doctrine, by the trickery of men, in the cunning craftiness of deceitful plotting," **(Ephesians 4:14 NKJV)**. The belt of truth protects us and prepares us for the battle that is part of every Christian's life. *rest your hope fully upon the grace that is to be brought to you.*

*"need truth counter "mind" procreation*

## The Vision
## The Human Pigsty

*And you will know  the Truth,  and  the Truth will set  you free. **(John 8:32)***

In this experience I was shown the results of the temptation of mankind living apart from the Holy Spirit. This was the most disgusting experience I could ever imagine. Some of it is too wicked and ugly to put into words. However there is a portion I can share.

*Now the works of the flesh are evident, which are: adultery, fornication, uncleanness, lewdness, idolatry, sorcery, hatred, contentions, jealousies, outbursts of wrath, selfish ambitions, dissensions, heresies, envy, murders, drunkenness, revelries, and the like; of which I tell you beforehand, just as I also told you in time past, that those who practice such things will not inherit the kingdom of God.* **(Galatians 5:19-21 NKJV)**

As this experience began, it was as if I was looking into a pigsty full of human beings wallowing in their sin because the resistance of the human flesh is so weak. It appeared as if quicksand was swallowing them up one by one. And all the while they were laughing and joking and inviting more people into this swampland of human waste. Only their heads and hands were visible which were so filthy and full of cruddy looking mud. The remainder of their bodies was buried beneath the swampy muck. I'm sorry to say but many of these were "so called Christians" and the temptations of their flesh were greater than the desire to bear witness to the cross. Galatians 5:17 says, *"For the flesh lusts against the Spirit, and the Spirit against the flesh; and these are contrary to one another, so that you do not do the things that you wish."*

Then suddenly I felt wet slimy black stuff under my feet. I was actually walking on top of this quicksand in the pigsty while many hands were reaching out and grabbing at my feet. They were trying to pull me down into pit with them. I'm startled but not afraid as I'm looking into the emptiness of their darkened hollow eyes. Then suddenly the hand of God reached down and tightened the belt of truth around my waist. And by this belt He lifted me up and out of this horrible experience. I breathed a sigh of relief.

However, to my surprise, He swung His arm around and began lowering me into another pigsty. Looking downward I could see the black slimy quicksand. This pit was even worse than the first one. The Lord said that this is reserved for the sexually immoral deviants including adulterers, homosexuals, LGBTQ, and those practicing bestiality. This was a horrible sight and smelled even worse. The stench of sexual immorality had reached the top of the vat. Their bodies were fully submerged in this miry muck with only their mouths and tongues exposed. There was no remorse or crying out for forgiveness. Instead they were uttering blasphemy and obscenities while many called on the names of their lovers. Indeed this was the most hideous, disgusting and repulsive thing I've ever seen. It was a hopeless situation and they didn't even realize it. Once more my belt was drawn even tighter and I was lifted out of this dreadful experience.

Immediately I knew God was tightening His belt of Truth around my waist. I was experiencing the full armor of God according to Ephesians 6:14-17. As Christians we are called to walk by faith and not by sight. **(2 Corinthians 5:7)** We are supposed to walk in the Way according to the Truth and demonstrate the Life of Jesus Christ. And at all times bear the fruit of the Spirit. **(Galatians 5:22-23)** In John 14:6 Jesus said that He is the Way, the Truth and the Life. He's talking about Himself.

# Greater Accountability

Christians are being called to a greater level of accountability. They can no longer get away with many of the things they used to. Too often sin is overlooked instead of being addressed. It's just not popular and if it's addressed it brings offense. Therefore over time sin becomes acceptable and embraced. In doing so we've turned our back on the truth. But Psalm 23:23 tells us to "buy the truth and sell it not;" not only that, but also get discernment and judgment, instruction and understanding. We have become politically correct and turned away from Scripture calling good evil and evil good.

I believe God is dealing with the sexually immoral on a greater level than ever before. I'm not saying that sexual immorality has been right or accepted by the Father in the past. No! I'm only saying that it is now being brought to the forefront and He is dealing with it. And those who participate in it will pay the penalty for their sin. In Romans 2:8 Paul said that those who are self-seeking *and* self-willed *and* disobedient to the Truth but responsive to wickedness, there will be indignation and wrath.

I believe that's why only the mouth of the people in the second pit was exposed. God in His mercy is giving them time to repent. However their conscience has been so seared that they cannot. I think Christians need to be praying for them. And if any Christian is a participant of this sin in any fashion, REPENT!

*The Lord is near to all who call upon Him, to all who call upon Him sincerely and in truth.* **(Psalm 145:18)**

I believe God is showing His children how to walk in truth and love. Love measures truth and truth measures love. You can't have one without the other. God is Love and He is also Truth. So you develop truth as you grow in the full measure of love. **(Ephesians 3:19)** And love increases as you grow in obedience to the Truth. It really is a simple equation.

## Led By The Spirit of Truth

The Truth will always lead you away from temptations of the flesh and into the path of righteousness. In Matthew 6 the Lord taught His disciples how to pray. Verse 13a is very interesting. It says, "And do not lead us into temptation, but deliver us from the evil one." I inquired of the Lord about this passage of scripture because He is the Way and the Truth so I don't believe the Lord would lead us into temptation. He took me to the account of Cain's conversation with God in Genesis 4. Cain is angry and depressed because God rejected his offering. And He asks Cain about his current state of mind. And here is the key to how we handle temptation. God said, "Sin crouches at your door; its desire is for you, but you must master it." And that is the correct response to every situation we encounter no matter how big or small. When sin comes knocking at the door of our mind (thoughts) we must say no!

*And the Lord said to Cain, Why are you angry? And why do you look sad and depressed and dejected? If you do well, will you not be accepted? And if you do not do well, sin crouches at your door; its desire is for you, but you must master it.* **(Genesis 4:76-7)**

The Lord is tightening His children's belt because they are being called into greater levels of intimacy with the Holy Spirit and accountability to the Father. We are told to know the Truth and it will <u>set us free</u> **(John 8:32)** and <u>John 16:13</u> says the <u>Spirit of Truth will guide us by His nature.</u>

*But when He, the Spirit of Truth (the Truth-giving Spirit) comes, He will guide you into all the Truth (the whole, full Truth). For He will not speak His own message [on His own authority]; but He will tell whatever He hears [from the Father; He will give the message that has been given to Him], and He will announce and declare to you the things that are to come [that will happen in the future].* **(John 16:13)**

In each of these experiences the Lord tightened my belt and pulled me out of the pit protecting me from the evil decay and filth of human desire. I believe He allowed me to see these awful sights to remind us that He is not blind to sin and also that we are responsible for the choices we make. We can't be flippant in our Christian walk and let the little foxes spoil our vineyard. **(SOS 2:15)** We must gird up our loins tightly each and every day and hold tight to the Spirit of Truth to guide us.

*Therefore put on God's complete armor, that you may be able to resist and stand your ground on the evil day [of danger], and, having done all [the crisis demands], to stand [firmly in your place]. Stand therefore [hold your ground], having tightened the belt of truth around your loins and having put on the breastplate of integrity and of moral rectitude and right standing with God, And having shod your feet in preparation [to face the enemy with the firm-footed stability, the promptness, and the readiness produced by the good news] of the Gospel of peace. Lift up over all the [covering] shield of saving faith, upon which you can quench all the flaming missiles of the wicked [one]. And take the helmet of salvation and the sword that the Spirit wields, which is the Word of God. (Ephesians 6:13-17)*

It's the Spirit of Truth's belt that girds our waist. And His belt delivers us from the pits of human filth. In this experience the Lord had a firm hand on my belt at all times and would not let me free from His grip. Because I place my faith and trust in Him He leads me on the path of righteousness for His name's sake and delivers me from temptation. The more I know the Truth the tighter the belt becomes because I've placed my faith in Him. Then He lifts me higher and places my feet on the solid Rock.

*God is Spirit, and those who worship Him must worship in spirit and truth." (John 4:24 NKJV)*

# God's Mercy

 *The Lord is merciful and gracious, slow to anger, and abounding in mercy. (Psalm 103:8 NKJV)*

I believe there's a line being drawn in the sand for the body of Christ. Many Christians are still dwelling in the land of loose living and up till now they've gotten away with it. They talk the talk but fail to walk the walk. Lusts of the flesh, lust of the eyes and pride of life still dominate their nature.

> *For all that is in the world—the lust of the flesh [craving for sensual gratification] and the lust of the eyes [greedy longings of the mind] and the pride of life [assurance in one's own resources or in the stability of earthly things]— these do not come from the Father but are from the world*
> 
> *[itself]. (1 John 2:16)*

I came away from this experience crying out to God for mercy for these people. The hopelessness in their eyes and their seared conscience were overwhelming. I believe Christians need to increase intercession for their loved ones. Many are still dabbling in the ways of the world and unless the desire of their heart changes they will be caught in the pigsty of human waste. I believe God is merciful and He's given plenty of time to repent but according to this dream, that portal of mercy is closing.

> *The Lord is slow to anger and great in power, and will not at all acquit the wicked. <u>The Lord has His way in the</u>*

*whirlwind and in the storm, and the clouds are the dust of His feet. (Nahum 1:3)*

According to Jeremiah 17:9, the heart is deceitful above all things, and it is exceedingly perverse and corrupt and severely, mortally sick! Who can know it [perceive, understand, be acquainted with his own heart and mind]? Therefore we should ask the Spirit of Truth to examine us daily. And if we are partakers of fleshly desires, repent and tighten the belt of truth. For all who are led by the Spirit of God are sons of God. **(Romans 8:14)** .

# Chapter Four
# The Year Of Patience
# The Pear

## Bob Jones' Revelation

In a trance many years ago, Bob Jones received the interpretation of Galatians 5:22-23. This experience took place during the time of Hanukkah. Bob saw people bringing baskets full of fruit to the Lord. Bob was told that the only gift you can give the Lord is the fruit of the Spirit. Because this fruit is worked into our spiritual nature as we mature in our Christian faith. In the course of this experience Bob was shown a natural fruit that coincides with the fruit of the Spirit. Each fruit is important to the Lord and as they were presented to Him, He blessed the giver of the gift.

> But the fruit of the Spirit is love, joy, peace, (patience) longsuffering, kindness, goodness, faithfulness, gentleness, self-control. Against such there is no law. **(Galatians 5:22-23 NKJV)**

Love was presented as the Orange, while Joy was presented to Him as a Peach, and the fruit of Peace was shown as an Apple. Patience or long suffering was presented to the Lord as a Pear, while the fruit of kindness is a Tomato. Strawberries were presented to the Lord, which represents Goodness, while Faithfulness came as the Grape. The fruit of Gentleness is the Banana.

The most difficult fruit of all is Self-Control and it was presented as the Grapefruit because this fruit can be both sweet and sour.

Bob would always say that the two most difficult fruits of the Spirit to attain were patience and self-control. I'm inclined to believe they are cousins. But if you can master one you'll master them both. It takes patience to maintain control of one's self and one must maintain control to remain patient. Cousins indeed!

I believe we are entering into a season where we will need to exercise a greater level of patience. We must be able to remain patient in spite of troubles and keep an even temper when unlikely circumstances arise. The church is now moving into the decade of being in "the rest of God." Therefore we must put our trust in the Lord and fear not! We are in this world but not of it so we must act accordingly. **(John 17:14-16)** I believe that when situations arise that are out of our control or contrary to our belief system, we need to take a deep breath and compose ourselves before speaking. We are accountable for every word we speak because our words have power. After all life and death are in the tongue. **(Proverbs 18:21)**

## Patient Endurance of Biblical Characters

Let's take a look at some biblical characters and some of the difficult situations they endured. Unlike today where all things are at our fingertips, they had to wait for everything. They un-

41

derstood patient endurance in a far greater measure than we could ever imagine. Many were called to endure great hardships in order to form their character. I believe each one developed a closer relationship with the Lord as they endured the testing of time. Often time's patience is simply keeping silent or bridling our tongue so as not to speak out of turn.

There are so many interesting characters in the Bible that faced one challenge after another. I wish there was time to mention more, however I've selected the ones the Lord highlighted to me. With each story I placed myself in their situation and wondered what I would have done. Today we have the Bible as our reference book. Unfortunately these men and women were writing the Book with their life.

I know that in my own life I've learned volumes through patient endurance. I've often said, "I have enough patience to be a well paid brain surgeon!" Joking of course. It's easy to be impatient when you are self-centered. But the more you crucify your flesh and trust the Lord you realize that He does work all things together for your good. **(Romans 8:28)** And when you seek first His kingdom **(Matthew 6:33)** and not your own, you can begin to rest in Him. Then patience will do a complete work in you.

*But let endurance and steadfastness and patience have full play and do a thorough work, so that you may be [people] perfectly and fully developed [with no defects], lacking in nothing. (James 1:4)*

Trust me, I am still a work in progress but I've come a long way. And every lesson I've learned along my journey has cost me something. But the rewards are so much greater than the sacrifice. What could I ever give in comparison to what our Lord gave for me? Nothing! If you can look to the joy that lies beyond the cross and take your focus off of your situation, you will master patient endurance. That's why our journey is called the road less traveled and the narrow way.

*But the gate is narrow (contracted by pressure) and the way is straightened and compressed that leads away to life, and few are those who find it. (Matthew 7:14)*

The road is narrow because with each commitment you make to the Lord you have to lay something down. And the farther you go the more narrow it becomes. Soon you will realize there's only room for the Lord and He's walking beside you.

# PART ONE
## Old Testament Characters
## And How They Endured with Patience

I've listed each biblical character according to their appearance in the Bible. Since there is no indication of the time Job lived, I've placed him first. After all, we've all heard about the patience of Job and hoped we would never have to be tested like he was.

# Job
## God Restored Double

Everyone's heard of the patience of Job and rightfully so. He was a man of integrity and righteous in the sight of God. Although the devil and Job's three so-called friends tested him, he did not sin. Throughout his trials of losing all of his livestock, servants, and everything he owned, he remained steadfast in God. I believe Job's greatest testing came upon his learning that all of his children were dead. Still he refused to curse or blame God. Even when Job was stricken with boils over his entire body, he remained humble before God. Job learned the lessons of patient endurance and reaped the rewards from the whirlwind. **(Job 42:4-5)** Through Job's faithfulness and complete trust in God all of his earthly possessions were restored twofold. And God blessed him with ten children.

*And the Lord turned the captivity of Job and restored his fortunes, when he prayed for his friends; also the Lord gave Job twice as much as he had before. (Job 42:10)*

# Noah
## Saves the Human Race

*Noah was a just and righteous man, blameless in his [evil] generation; Noah walked [in habitual fellowship] with God. (Genesis 6:9b)*

44

Noah lived in an evil time when the whole earth was filled with violence and corruption. Yet he did not allow the evil standards of his day to rob him of fellowship with God. Noah walked with God and therefore God chose him to accomplish a tremendous task. Building an ark to the exact specifications was by itself challenging and time consuming. He didn't have all the modern equipment that's available to us today.

Building the ark took approximately 120 years. Talk about being patient. All the while he was being mocked and ridiculed by wicked revelers, he remained a preacher of righteousness. Noah's patient endurance saved his whole family. After the flood God blessed Noah and restored the creation command, "Be fruitful and multiply and fill the earth." **(Genesis 9:1)**

*And He spared not the ancient world, but preserved Noah, a preacher of righteousness, with seven other persons, when He brought a flood upon the world of ungodly [people]. (2 Peter 2:5)*

The faithful prayers of the saints can preserve the whole family. Sometimes it takes many years of praying for loved ones before we see the fruit of our labors. It takes prayer, faith, trust and patient endurance to see positive results but the rewards are well worth the wait.

# Abraham
# Father of Many Nations

God promised Abraham that he would be the father of many nations. **(Genesis 12:1-3)** At that time he and his wife Sarah had no children. Yet God continued to reinforce His promise to Abraham throughout the years **(Genesis 13:6; 15:1-6; 17:6-8; 18:10)**. Although Abraham fathered a son named Ishmael by Sarah's handmaiden, he remained hopeful of the Lord's promise.

Finally when Abraham was 100 and Sarah was 90 years old and well beyond child bearing, God gave them Isaac, their son of promise. Though it took years of patiently waiting, they received the promise of God. Hebrews 6:15 say of Abraham, "And so, after he had patiently endured, he obtained the promise."

Abraham's greatest testing of faith and patience came when God asked him to offer Isaac as a sacrifice on the altar. His heart must have sunk, but only for a moment. How could he become the father of many nations without the promised son Isaac to reproduce? His journey up the mountain must have seemed like an eternity. And Abraham stretched forth his hand and took hold of the knife to slay his son. *But the Angel of the Lord called to him from heaven and said, Abraham, Abraham! He answered, Here I am. And He said, Do not lay your hand on the lad or do anything to him; for now I know that you fear and revere God, since you have not held back from Me or begrudged giving Me your son, your only son.* **(Genesis 22:10-12)**

Although God promised Abraham many years earlier that he would be the father of many nations, it wasn't till after this final testing of his faith and long-suffering that he received the blessing. Often times there's a long wait between the promise and receiving the fulfillment. In the time between the two, God builds our character. Obedience is key to character building.

*In blessing I will bless you and in multiplying I will multiply your descendants like the stars of the heavens and like the sand on the seashore. And your Seed (Heir) will possess the gate of His enemies, and in your Seed [Christ] shall all the nations of the earth be blessed and [by Him] bless themselves, because you have heard and obeyed My voice.* **(Genesis 2:17-18)**

## Joseph
## A Picture of Patience

Joseph's life is a picture of patience. His brothers threw him into a pit and later sold him as a slave **(Genesis 37:27, 28)**. He was taken to Egypt and sold to Potiphar, an officer of the pharaoh. Potiphar's wife accused him of a crime he didn't commit and Joseph was then placed in prison for thirteen years. He was even forgotten by his fellow inmate whom he prophesied his release from prison and promotion. Though he did not understand all that was happening, he trusted God to work out His plan in His time.

Joseph patiently worked faithfully in each situation he was in. He waited for God to fulfill His promise of leadership that was shown him as a child through his dreams. Joseph knew he would become a leader of his people **(Genesis 37:5-11)**. He had to be patient, as he believed God, but probably wondered why he was sitting in a prison cell.

After many long years in prison Pharaoh called upon Joseph to interpret his dreams. Joseph called upon his God and trusted Him for the understanding. Pharaoh immediately appointed him second in command over all Egypt saving it from devastation through famine.

Patience was needed to allow God to accomplish His purposes in the life of Joseph and his family. And Joseph knew that through patient endurance not only Egypt was saved but also his whole family was preserved. Joseph's life is a picture of hope for all of us. He literally went from the pit to the prison to the palace.

*God sent me before you to preserve for you posterity and to continue a remnant on the earth, to save your lives by a great escape and save for you many survivors.*
***(Genesis 45:7)***

# Moses
# God's Deliverer

Moses was the child of a Hebrew slave but found and raised by the Pharaoh's daughter. He spent the first forty years of his life in Pharaoh's court. Although he was nurtured in the customs of the Egyptians, Hebrew blood flowed through his veins. While defending a Hebrew slave he killed an Egyptian. After burying him in the sand he fled Egypt for Midian. **(Exodus 2:12)** There he would marry a Midianite woman and spend the next forty years being a shepherd and learning survival skills in the Sinai desert. God set a plan in motion. Moses was being prepared to lead the Israelite children out of bondage. Then one day Moses had an encounter with a burning bush **(Exodus 3:1-12)** and received his commissioning to return to Egypt and tell the pharaoh "Let My people go!"

By now Moses was eighty years old and just getting started. After many meetings with pharaoh and God sending ten plagues, pharaoh finally agreed to release the children of Israel from bondage. Can you imagine the patience Moses had to endure? He had to travel with approximately 600,000 men, besides women and children for forty years. **(Exodus 12:37)** And all the while they grumbled and complained about one thing or another. They were rarely content and time after time they wanted to return to Egypt. They grew weary and didn't want to hear God's voice. Although they promised to obey the law they grew impatient and built a golden calf to worship. God was provoked to anger and wanted to destroy all of them but Moses and Aaron interceded on their behalf.

Faith, trust, humility, patience, obedience and fear of the Lord describe some of Moses' attributes. However he was a true friend of God and met with Him face to face. In my opinion he endured more than any other biblical character and over a longer period of time. He had the highest calling of all men and with the higher calling greater obedience is required. When he disobeyed the Lord it cost both himself and Aaron the privilege of going into the Promised Land. They were told to speak to the rock and it would bring forth water, however, they struck the rock like they did once before. God called their disobedience rebellion. Aaron was stripped of his priestly garments and died on Mount Hor. His son Eleazar replaced him as high priest. **(Numbers 20:23-29)**

*Take the rod, and assemble the congregation, you and Aaron your brother, and tell the rock before their eyes to give forth its water, and you shall bring forth to them water out of the rock; so you shall give the congregation and their livestock drink. So Moses took the rod from before the Lord, as He commanded him. And Moses and Aaron assembled the congregation before the rock and Moses said to them, Hear now, you rebels; must we bring you water out of this rock? And Moses lifted up his hand and with his rod he smote the rock twice. And the water came out abundantly, and the congregation drank, and their livestock. And the Lord said to Moses and Aaron, Because you did not believe in (rely on, cling to) Me to sanctify Me in the eyes of the Israelites, you therefore shall not bring this congregation into the land which I have given them. (Numbers 20:8-12)*

Moses was 120 years old when he died; his eye was not dim nor his natural force abated. Although he would not enter the Promised Land, God took him to Mount Nebo and allowed him to see it from afar. Indeed Moses was long-suffering for a good cause. He was blessed more than any other man on earth; he met with God face-to-face daily. He was God's friend and deliverer. He truly walked with God.

*And the Lord said to him, this is the land, which I swore to Abraham, Isaac, and Jacob, saying, I will give it to your descendants. I have let you see it with your eyes, but you shall not go over there. So Moses the servant of the Lord died there in the land of Moab, according to the word of the Lord, and He buried him in the valley of the land of Moab opposite Beth-peor, but no man knows where his tomb is to this day. Moses was 120 years old when he died; his eye was not dim nor his natural force abated.* **(Deuteronomy 34:4-7)**

## King David
## God's Chosen King

David was Jesse's eighth son and in the sight of man didn't measure up to kingly status but God knew this young man's heart. David loved God and had a warrior spirit. He worshipped God and trusted Him in everything. One day God sent the prophet Samuel to anoint him king. David was about seventeen **(1 Samuel 16)** however he would not take the throne until he was thirty. Talk about patient endurance. Not only did David have to wait, he had to serve Saul when an evil spirit tormented him.

> *But the Spirit of the Lord departed from Saul, and an evil spirit from the Lord tormented and troubled him. And when the evil spirit from God was upon Saul, David took a lyre and played it; so Saul was refreshed and became well, and the evil spirit left him. (1 Samuel 16:14 & 23)*

In time Saul would grow jealous of David and desire his death. David had to flee to the mountains and run for his life. Yet all the while his heart remained tender toward God. After thirteen years of enduring Saul's temper tantrums and schemes, David took his rightful position as King of Israel. **(2 Samuel 5:1-2)**

## The Shunammite
## Faithful Endurance

One of my favorite stories is that of the Shunammite in 2 Kings 4:25-37. It gives the account of the Shunammite woman whose young child had sunstroke and died in her arms. She laid the lad on the bed prepared for Elisha in the upper room of her house. Then she journeyed to Mt. Carmel to ask Elisha to return with her. The trip from Shunam to Mt. Carmel was approximately 40 miles round trip and she had to travel by donkey. It probably took more than a day just to get there. Her heart was vexed when she finally reached the prophet. **(Verse 27)** I believe this woman displayed great faith in God and trust in the prophet who prophesied the birth of this child. The Shunammite woman is a clear picture of patient endurance. Her heart filled with joy as Elisha raised him from death to life.

*Then he returned and walked in the house to and fro and went up again and stretched himself upon him. And the child sneezed seven times, and then opened his eyes. Then [Elisha] called Gehazi and said, call this Shunammite. So he called her. And when she came, he said, take up your son. She came and fell at his feet, bowing herself to the ground. Then she took up her son and went out.* **(2 Kings 4:35-37)**

## PART TWO
### New Testament Characters
### And How They Endured with Patience

### Elizabeth and Zacharias
### Endured Through Silence

*There was in the days of Herod, the king of Judea, a certain priest named Zacharias, of the division of Abijah. His wife was of the daughters of Aaron, and her name was Elizabeth. And they were both righteous before God, walking in all the commandments and ordinances of the Lord blameless. But they had no child, because Elizabeth was barren, and they were both well advanced in years.* **(Luke 1:5-7)**

There is no indication of either Elizabeth or Zacharias age however the scripture says they were both advanced in years and Elizabeth was barren. And now the angel Gabriel visited Zacharias announcing the birth of their son John and the calling on his life. **(Luke 1:11-20)** I think their hope for having children had long passed. Because of Zacharias' unbelief, he's struck dumb.

*Now behold, you will be and will continue to be silent and not able to speak till the day when these things take place, because you have not believed what I told you; but my words are of a kind which will be fulfilled in the appointed and proper time. (Luke 1:20)*

Elizabeth and Zachariah had to ride this test of patient endurance out together. She became pregnant at an old age and would birth the child who would be the forerunner of the Messiah. And Zachariah remained mute until the circumcision of his long awaited son. His final testing of faith was in naming his son. Elizabeth had already announced his name would be John but now her husband needed to agree. Since he couldn't speak he asked for a writing tablet. When he wrote, "His name is John" his tongue was loosed and he began to speak and praise the Lord.

*Then Zachariah asked for a writing tablet and wrote, his name is John. And they were all astonished. And at once his mouth was opened and his tongue loosed, and he began to speak, blessing and praising and thanking God. (Luke 1:63-64)*

Many times we are put to the test of silence. And often times it's hard to keep quiet on a matter. But all things must be in God's timing or it can delay or even abort the plan of the Holy Spirit. Our flesh desires its own way and can cause us to speak out of turn. Patience is a virtue and I believe that if we can't bridle our tongue on our own, God will assist us. It's a working of patience, obedience and humility working through us to bridle our tongue and bring it into agreement with the Lord.

## Jesus
## Endured Patience With Joy

Jesus was the most patient man that ever lived on the face of the earth. He endured every temptation that mankind is tempted with yet He never sinned. **(Hebrews 4:15)** He endured forty days in the wilderness without food or water. At the end of this time and when He was weak the devil tempted Him. Satan offered Him food, riches and all the glory of the world still He did not sin. He spoke the Word of God and said to the devil, *"Get behind Me, Satan!" (Luke 4:8)*

*Then Jesus, full of and controlled by the Holy Spirit, returned from the Jordan and was led in [by] the [Holy] Spirit. For (during) forty days in the wilderness (desert), He was tempted (tried, tested exceedingly) by the devil. And He ate nothing during those days, and when they were completed, He was hungry.*

*Then the devil said to Him, if You are the Son of God, order this stone to turn into a loaf [of bread]. And Jesus replied to him, it is written, Man shall not live and be sustained by (on) bread alone but by every word and expression of God.*

*Then the devil took Him up to a high mountain and showed Him all the kingdoms of the habitable world in a moment of time [in the twinkling of an eye]. And he said to Him, to You I will give all this power and authority and their glory (all their magnificence, excellence, preeminence, dignity, and grace), for it has been turned over to me, and I give it to whomever I will. Therefore if You will do homage to and worship me [just once], it shall all be Yours. And Jesus replied to him, get behind Me, Satan! It is written, you shall do homage to and worship the Lord your God, and Him only shall you serve.*

*Then he took Him to Jerusalem and set Him on a gable of the temple, and said to Him, if You are the Son of God, cast Yourself down from here; for it is written, He will give His angels charge over you to guard and watch over you closely and carefully; and on their hands they will bear you up, lest you strike your foot against a stone.*

*And Jesus replied to him, [The Scripture] says, you shall not tempt (try, test exceedingly) the Lord your God. And when the devil had ended every [the complete cycle of] temptation, he [temporarily] left Him [that is, stood off from Him] until another more opportune and favorable time. (Luke 4:1-13)*

Jesus patiently endured the constant harassment from the Pharisees, Sadducees and many of the common people who opposed Him. They were constantly badgering Him and trying to find ways to cause Him to falter. And daily He endured the challenges of His own disciples. Throughout every trial, test and temptation He walked in perfect obedience to the Father. He endured the scourging and bore the shame of the cross for our sake. Yet even in His pain and shame He spoke not a word and did not sin.

*Surely He has borne our griefs and carried our sorrows; yet we esteemed Him stricken, smitten by God, and afflicted. But He was wounded for our transgressions, He was bruised for our iniquities; the chastisement for our peace was upon Him, and by His stripes we are healed.* **(Isaiah 53:4-5 NKJV)**

The author of Hebrews says it best. *Jesus, the author and finisher of our faith, who for the joy that was set before Him endured the cross, despising the shame, and has sat down at the right hand of the throne of God.* **(Hebrews 12:2 NKJV)** Our Lord and Savior finished His earthly life as the spotless Lamb of God for our sake. We are the joy that was set before Him and He endured everything for us. So let us run with endurance the race that is set before us, **(Hebrews 12:1b)** giving honor to the author and finisher of our faith.

# Gadarene Demoniac
## Endured Patience While Tormented

Mark 5:1-20 gives the account of the demoniac who was possessed by a legion of demons and lived in the graveyard. Chains and handcuffs could not hold him and he was heard day and night screaming and would often cut himself with stones. Yet when Jesus came to that region the demoniac fell on his knees in honor of the Son of God. There's no record of how long he was possessed but apparently long enough that everyone feared him. He was cast out of society, naked and worst of all tormented continuously.

When Jesus cast the demons out of him and sent them into a herd of hogs, people were struck with fear and unbelief. The man who had a legion of demons now had a sound mind. He wanted to join Jesus but the Lord had other plans for him. This man would become a great evangelist in Decapolis, the region of ten cities.

> *But Jesus refused to permit him, but said to him, go home to your own [family and relatives and friends] and bring back word to them of how much the Lord has done for you, and [how He has] had sympathy for you and mercy on you. And he departed and began to publicly proclaim in Decapolis [the region of the ten cities] how much Jesus had done for him, and all the people were astonished and marveled. (Mark 5:19-20)*

I believe the demoniac could have committed suicide at any time. He was demon possessed and had superhuman strength. Yet I believe he heard about this man named Jesus and held on to the hope that He would present Himself in his region. Day and night he cried out in torment beckoning his deliverance. Then one day the Lord came calling and set the demoniac free. Enduring this test was painful on many levels however the reward was far greater and well worth the wait.

*Therefore if the Son makes you free, you shall be free indeed.* **(John 8:36 NKJV)**

## Woman With Issue of Blood
## Physical Endurance

Talk about patient endurance. How about the woman with the issue of blood? She sought help from every doctor in the region for twelve years. And to no avail. She was long-suffering in a physical way yet never gave up hope. She spent all of her money seeking a cure and her condition worsened. But when she heard that the Healer was in town she pressed through the crowd and touched the hem of His garment. Immediately she was healed.

*And there was a woman who had had a flow of blood for twelve years, and who had endured much suffering under [the hands of] many physicians and had spent all that she had, and was no better but instead grew worse. She had heard the reports concerning Jesus, and she came up be-*

*hind Him in the throng and touched His garment, For she kept saying, If I only touch His garments, I shall be restored to health. And immediately her flow of blood was dried up at the source, and [suddenly] she felt in her body that she was healed of her [distressing] ailment. **(Mark 5:25-29)***

*And He said to her, Daughter, your faith (your trust and confidence in Me, springing from faith in God) has restored you to health. Go in (into) peace and be continually healed and freed from your (distressing bodily) disease. **(Mark 5:34)***

## Prodigal Son's Father
## Restoration Through Patience

Many times I've read the story of the prodigal son and how he was greedy and wanted his inheritance early. So his father complied. The son began the journey of his life that left him homeless and literally destitute. When famine hit the land he ended up working and living with hogs. He was a mess to say the least. In his brokenness he decided to go home to his father and ask forgiveness. He was hoping his father would make him like a hired hand.

*I will get up and go to my father, and I will say to him, Father, I have sinned against heaven and in your sight. I am no longer worthy to be called your son; [just] make me like one of your hired servants. **(Luke 15:18-19)***

I believe this father longed in his heart for his son's return. I can see him standing on the hillside everyday with expectation of his son coming over the rise of the hill. Then one-day joy filled his heart when at last his eyes beheld his son. Patience healed the father's heart and returned his son to the Lord. The son learned repentance through long-suffering and unconditional love through his father's open arms.

*So he got up and came to his [own] father. But while he was still a long way off, his father saw him and was moved with pity and tenderness [for him]; and he ran and embraced him and kissed him [fervently]. (Luke 15:20)*

# PART THREE

## The Heavenly Host Are
## Still Patiently Waiting

### God the Father

No one has been more patient than our Heavenly Father. Since the fall of man He has waited for mankind to come back into union with Him. Complete fellowship has never been established on earth as it is in heaven. We have all sinned and fallen short of the glory of God. **(Romans 3:23)** His righteous and precious glory has been misunderstood and misused over the centuries. But the Father loves His children and patiently awaits a perfect union with them.

*The Lord does not delay and is not tardy or slow about what He promises, according to some people's conception of slowness, but He is long-suffering (extraordinarily patient) toward you, not desiring that any should perish, but that all should turn to repentance. (2 Peter 3:9)*

The Father patiently waited until the appointed time in history to send His Son to the earth to redeem mankind from sin. Again He waited patiently thirty-three years until the Son would return to His heavenly home. And once again the Father waits for the time He will send His precious Son to earth the second time to gather His saints unto Himself.

## Great Cloud of Witnesses

Throughout history there have been many precious saints who served the Lord with all of their heart. Each one in his/her way prepared the road that we now travel. Some were preachers or teachers that taught the flock to the best of their ability according to the knowledge of the Word they understood. Were there mistakes along the way? Yes and probably many but this did not distract them from their purpose of presenting the gospel of the good news. Many were circuit riders that traveled long, hard treacherous terrain by horseback for months or years at a time spreading the good news. Some were evangelists that pitched their tent in many towns across this and other nations to deliver the good news and winning souls to Christ. Apostles began forming the government of God while prophets prophesied the coming King. And understanding of the gifts of the Holy Spirit became evident as the five-fold ministry was established. Still many endured the road less traveled and were martyred for the sake of the gospel.

*Therefore then, since we are surrounded by so great a cloud of witnesses [who have borne testimony to the Truth], let us strip off and throw aside every encumbrance (unnecessary weight) and that sin which so readily (deftly and cleverly) clings to and entangles us, and let us run with patient endurance and steady and active persistence the appointed course of the race that is set before us, Looking away [from all that will distract] to Jesus, Who is the Leader and the Source of our faith [giving the first incentive for our belief] and is also its Finisher [bringing it to maturity and perfection].* **(Hebrews 12:1-2a)**

Each one of these forerunners borne testimony to the Truth and went home to Jesus without seeing the fulfillment of their calling. They were all part of the great cloud of witnesses who ran their race with patient endurance for the higher calling in Christ. However their testimony is not complete without ours. Together we form a tapestry of the Father's handiwork.

*And all of these, though they won divine approval by [means of] their faith, did not receive the fulfillment of what was promised, because God had us in mind and had something better and greater in view for us, so that they [these heroes and heroines of faith] should not come to*

*perfection apart from us [before we could join them].*
*(Hebrews 11:39-40)*

Every Christian is important to God and each one had a part in preparing the way for the next generation. Many were church leaders while countless many more were simply parents and grandparents. They loved the Lord and never stopped praying for and teaching their family about Jesus. A witness is just that, a witness to the testimony of Jesus in their life. No one needs a platform to share Jesus; our life is His testimony.

## Angels That Gather

Throughout scripture we've seen angels on assignment; Daniel, Virgin Mary and Zacharias each had encounters with mighty angels of God. Angels are sent on assignment at appointed times to accomplish a mission designated by the Father. In Matthew 13:41 the Lord said, *"The Son of Man will send forth His angels, and they will gather out of His kingdom all causes of offense (persons by whom others are drawn into error or sin) and all who do iniquity and act wickedly.* I believe there is a company of angles that have been patiently waiting over two thousand years for the release of their assignment. As the end of the age draws nearer, more angels are being released.

We are witnessing lawlessness on a scale like we've never seen before, however the enemy is being exposed at every corner. Angels are removing every cause of offense that would prevent salvation from coming forth. I believe we are going to see more and more obstacles removed as the gospel is revealed on a greater scale. Angels must be released to help the saints reap the harvest fields. Then the plowman shall overcome the reaper and we will experience an unending harvest.

*Behold, the days are coming, says the Lord, that the plowman shall overtake the reaper, and the treader of grapes him who sows the seed; and the mountains shall drop sweet wine and all the hills shall melt [that is, everything heretofore barren and unfruitful shall overflow with spiritual blessing]. (**Amos 9:13**)*

# PART FOUR

## Lessons From History
## Needed for Today

## Moses and Aaron
## A Parable of Today's Leadership

We've looked at many biblical characters and how they endured long-suffering through various circumstances they faced. Some like Noah and Moses endured for a lengthy time while others in comparison only a short while. The length of time spent is not the important issue. It's the attitude and response to the situation. Were they Christ like in nature or self-centered? Hebrews 12:2b says that Christ, for the joy [of obtaining the prize] that was set before Him, endured the cross, despising and ignoring the shame. He endured the cross for our benefit. We are His prize and His joy. He is now seated at the right hand of the throne of God.

I believe we must learn a lesson from Moses and Aaron. These two brothers served God with all of their heart for forty years. Aaron was the high priest and spokesman for Moses to the people. Moses is the only man to have ever met with God face to face. For forty years they both spent endless hours in the presence of God yet neither one entered the Promised Land. Why? Numbers 20:24 says that they rebelled against God. It might seem like a little "oops I forgot" to us. But it was a big deal to the Father. He expects His children to be obedient. Had they grown familiar with His voice? Did they simply forget what He said? Had they grown weary from hearing the Israelites complaints? I believe their impatience caused them to become provoked with them therefore striking the rock in anger instead of speaking to it as commanded by God.

This one act of disobedience caused Aaron to be stripped of his priestly garments. And I believe this is a parable or shadow of things to come in the church today. Too many have gotten away with too much for too long. To those God has given greater authority, greater obedience is required. **(Luke 12:48)** There's been a half-hearted, lackadaisical attitude hovering over the church at large for a long time. Leaders are called to lead the sheep not fall asleep on the job. I believe God is calling them out in this season. They are either going to stand up and be counted among the faithful or be stripped of their priestly garments.

*Aaron shall be gathered to his people. For he shall not enter the land which I have given to the Israelites, because you both rebelled against My instructions at the waters of Meribah. Take Aaron and Eleazar his son and bring them up to Mount Hor. **(Numbers 20:23-25)***

Replacements, like Aaron's son Eleazar and Joshua, Moses' assistant, are waiting in the wings. They were men God anointed to lead Israel's remnant into the Promised Land. Now in the same way today God has anointed sons and daughters that will take the reins and bring the body into the promises of yes and amen. And there will be no delay because the day of the church's mourning is over.

*Strip Aaron of his vestments and put them on Eleazar his son, and Aaron shall be gathered to his people, and shall die there. And Moses did as the Lord commanded; and they went up Mount Hor in the sight of all the congregation. And Moses stripped Aaron of his [priestly] garments and put them on Eleazar his son. And Aaron died there on the mountain top; and Moses and Eleazar came down from the mountain. When all the congregation saw that Aaron was dead, they wept and mourned for him thirty days, all the house of Israel. **(Numbers 20:26-29)***

# Isaac and Rebekah
# Preserved the Promised Seed

Within Genesis 24 lies a beautiful love story illustrative of God the Father who sends forth His Holy Spirit to prepare a bride for His Son. After Sarah's death, Abraham sends his faithful servant Eliezer to his brother Nahor's camp to find a wife for his son Isaac. She had to be a pure and chaste virgin and willing to leave her family at once. The faithful servant Eliezer remains obedient, patient and full of praise for his master Abraham. God answered his prayer and sends Rebekah to the well to greet him and his camels giving them water. **(verse 14)** The servant then adorns her with jewelry and later meets with her father and brother. He remains humble and won't even eat until he shares the purpose of his coming to Nahor. Immediately Nahor **(verse 51)** gives Eliezer permission to take Rebekah with him as a wife for his master's son.

The following day Rebekah leaves with Eliezer on a forty-day journey to meet her intended husband Isaac. All the while she's being told about the child of promise and the inheritance of Abraham's seed. After all Eliezer had to place his hand under Abraham's groin as an oath to protect the promised seed of his loin. **(verse 2)** Because Isaac was the child of promise the inheritance would come through him and his descendants. And this is the same blessing Rebekah's family gave her upon her departure.

*And they blessed Rebekah and said to her, you are our sister; may you become the mother of thousands of ten thou-*

*sands, and let your posterity possess the gate of their ene-mies. (Genesis 24:60)*

It was prophesied that Rebekah would become the mother of ten thousands, or many nations. This was Abraham's promise that could only come through his son Isaac. **(Genesis 22:17)** But here is where their patient endurance began. Isaac was forty years old when he married Rebekah **(Genesis 25:20)** and sixty years old when his twin sons Jacob and Esau were born. **(Genesis 25:26)** As a couple they sought God about the promised seed that would come through their union. Unlike Sarah and Abraham, they waited on God to provide instead of seeking the help from her handmaiden Hagar. **(Genesis 16:3-15)** So for twenty long years they prayed, trusted God and waited for a child. And when God answered their prayers, He blessed them with two sons, Esau the first-born and his twin brother Jacob. But through Jacob, the second-born twelve tribes would be born whose descendants would be innumerable. **(Genesis 17)**

God is always faithful to His promises and we must co-labor with Him. Many times patience is our labor. As you can see from this beautiful story God paid double the dividends. I believe Isaac learned a lesson from his father's mistake. Isaac understood that he was the promised child and therefore honored God with his life. After all, he endured the testing of his father who was willing to sacrifice him on the altar. I believe Isaac was the first fruit of Abraham's faithfulness. Just like Abraham's faithful servant sought a chaste virgin for his son, today the Holy Spirit is seeking those who will be faithful to the promised seed. He's looking for those who will patiently endure even when they don't see results for many years. He's looking for those who will seek His face despite the circumstance and not seek another way to accomplish the task set before them. I believe this precious story is one of hope through patient endurance knowing that God is faithful to fulfill His promises no matter how long it takes.

Here's something I find interesting. Rebekah knew that she was pregnant with two sons after she inquired of the Lord. He told her that the older son would serve the younger one. **(Genesis 25:22-24)** I believe she held that promise in her heart because she was still protecting the promised seed of Abraham whose lineage traces back to Adam and therefore God. **(Luke 3:23)** I view Rebekah as a forerunner to Mary the mother of our Lord.

*[Two] children struggled together within her; and she said, if it is so [that the Lord has heard our prayer], why am I like this? And she went to inquire of the Lord. The Lord said to her, [The founders of] two nations are in your womb, and the separation of two peoples has begun in your body; the one people shall be stronger than the other, and the elder shall serve the younger. When her days to be delivered were fulfilled, behold, there were twins in her womb. (Genesis 25:22-24)*

In time when Isaac was old and his eyesight very poor, Rebekah helped Jacob deceive his father. **(Genesis 27)** Therefore Isaac gave Jacob the blessing of the first-born son and eventually the twelve tribes of Israel were birthed through him. Of course Jacob himself had to wait fourteen years and endure his father-in-law Laban's demands as payment for Rachel as his wife. **(Genesis 30)** I believe Abraham's entire lineage had to endure patiently to preserve the promised seed. As each generation was tested they remembered important results from their ancestors' patience and impatient experiences.

*Therefore it is of faith that it might be according to grace, so that the promise might be sure to all the seed, not only to those who are of the law, but also to those who are of the faith of Abraham, who is the father of us all (as it is written, "I have made you a father of many nations") in the presence of Him whom he believed—God, who gives life to the dead and calls those things which do not exist as though they did; who, contrary to hope, in hope believed, so that he became the father of many nations, according to what was spoken, "So shall your descendants be. (Romans 4:16-18NKJV)*

Since Abraham is considered the father of our faith and we are his spiritual offspring that receive the blessings of the first-born, let us hold tight to the reins that have been handed down through the generations. Let us strip off and throw aside every encumbrance (unnecessary weight) and that sin which so readily (deftly and cleverly) clings to and entangles us, and let us run with patient endurance and steady and active persistence the appointed course of the race that is set before us, **(Hebrews 12:1)** What we do in our lifetime prepares the way for the following generation. Let us patiently look unto Jesus, the author and finisher of our faith, who for the joy that was set before

Him endured the cross. **(Hebrews 12:2a)** Let us do our part to preserve the seed of the Father for the next generation.

## Three Vital Keys
## To Patient Endurance

Each of these aforementioned characters conformed to the will of God. Through Abraham and Sarah's impatience a son was born of a bondwoman. Their disobedience prolonged the birth of their child of promise. It took another thirteen years of patient endurance for God's will to be made perfect. My prayer for all Christians is that we could face every situation with joy in our heart. And seek God for the purpose of each trial and what we can learn from it. The lesson we acquire from the trial we endure will help us to prepare others and save them from falling into the enemy's trap. Remember we are all one body and need to help one another. That's why these biblical examples are so important. Let's embrace each trial with an open mind and love in our heart.

*I therefore, the prisoner for the Lord, appeal to and beg you to walk (lead a life) worthy of the [divine] calling to which you have been called [with behavior that is a credit to the summons to God's service, living as becomes you] with complete lowliness of mind (humility) and meekness (unselfishness, gentleness, mildness), with patience, bearing with one another and making allowances because you love one another. (Ephesians 4:1-2)*

Three vital keys that will help lessen the time of endurance are humility, obedience and trust. Remain humble while seeking His will for direction and understanding. Obey quickly whatever He asks you to do and do it with a spirit of excellence as unto the Lord. And trust the Lord in all things. He will never ask you to do something that He hasn't already given you the grace to do.

# Chapter Five
# Gold Mine Snippets

I saved this section for last because each revelation was very short and clear. Therefore I call them snippets. Bob would call them a trance. In each one the Lord gave me understanding and/or spoke to me regarding it therefore I'm choosing not to add anything to them. They are clear and precise, no fluff!

## Worship Leaders Like Keith Green

Worship leaders are going to sing praises unto the Lord not man. I was shown that artists like Keith Green, who the devil killed before his time has written songs in heaven. Green, along with eleven others including two of his small children, died in a plane crash on July 28, 1982, near Lindale, Texas. Keith was a Christian songwriter and musician devoted to evangelism through worship. His life was cut short. He was just twenty-eight years old at the time of his death. Green and other prophetic voices have written these songs in heaven. They've been reserved for a people who will worship God in the midst of the congregation and not be influenced by man.

The Lord showed me musicians that quit worshiping once they had families because life on the road got too tough. They basically packed up their tents and quit. Now they serve man through nonspiritual means. They walked away from their first love "music". But He has not forgotten them and He's wooing their heart of passion for Him. He's restoring them to first love "Jesus". Once again they will praise Him but from a new perspective. They are not abandoning the family, instead they're including them as they worship Him and the entire world shall see. After all, family is important to God.

Get ready to see worship leaders emerge with new songs and passion for Jesus. No longer will they look to man for approval because their heart is totally abandoned to the Lord. They will worship like King David as the tabernacle of David is restored to its glory. And the glory of God will flow freely out of a passionate heart abandoned before the Lord. God is not looking for professional musicians; He's looking for laid down lovers that will worship Him in spirit and truth.

After all, all lyrics originate in heaven. However much of it gets distorted as it goes through the second heaven. Then when the revelation reaches earth what is meant to be a worship song carnal man turns it into country, pop, rock, rap or jazz. Take for example "My Sweet Lord" by George Harrison of the Beatle fame. This is a beautiful song and you think he's singing about Jesus. Then you listen to the background singers and they are singing the names of Hindu gods such as Krishna, a major deity in Hinduism, and Maheshwara, the supreme god who is one of the main deities of Hinduism. So who is the lord Harrison was singing about? And when we join in with singing it, we are worshiping his Hindu gods also. Therefore I believe that what God meant to be a love song from His children, man distorted and contaminated the words. And Christians as well as the world embraced it. We haven't been listening.

But get ready as new songs are released from heaven. Soon anointed men and women who are not willing to compromise or take the glory for them- selves will receive them. These chosen ones will face the wall so not to bring attention to themselves. They will lead the body of Christ into the holiness of the Lord and bow down to worship God.

## Female Voices Anointed

I was shown the anointing coming on female voices. In the dream there were two men and one woman singing together. The anointing was so strong on the woman that she had to hold back her voice so as not to drown out the men. In humility she restrained her voice but once the men recognized the anointing they stepped aside and let her continue. When she sang the whole earth vibrated. Now the scene changed and we received a phone call from a young girl. She called to inform us that her dad got saved and healed when he heard this woman sing.

I believe female singers, worship leaders and speakers are com- ing to the forefront in this season. The anointing on their voice is undeniable. As they remain humble God will exalt them. And from this place of honoring Him we will experience salvation as well as healing.

*Humble yourselves in the sight of the Lord, and He will lift you up. (James 4:10 NKJV)*

I believe we're going to see whole congregations set free through the power of the word released under the anointing. It's not the volume it's the value of the word. It doesn't matter if it's spoken or sung. Miracles are in the midst as God's glory rests upon His people. I'm expecting Sunday services and other meetings to be different in the future. Some meetings will turn into worship alone as the anointing touches the worship team. Abandoned hearts will find themselves engaged and face down on the floor in prayer. Leaders will harken to the Holy Spirit and not quench His voice. It's going to be a new day in the church at large as they drop their programs and agendas to flow with the Holy Spirit. The church at large has been trying to fit Him into their program instead of being led by Him. It's a new dynamic but we are going to witness the humility of many.

## Pay Attention To Children

I was shown many children who had prophetic experiences. Yet when they shared them with their parents, teachers or other adults were totally ignored or made fun of.

One vision I had was that of a young brother and sister, perhaps seven or eight years old. They had the same experience where they were shown that two devastating earthquakes were going to take place where they lived. But when they shared it with their parents, they laughed it off and ignored them. They even accused them of making it up saying it must have been a movie they watched.

Then the Lord spoke to me saying, "This is a warning! People aren't listening to the children. If they listened they would save the whole family, but pride won't allow them to hear. Children are giving accurate prophecies and adults need to listen to them."

I have noticed that my young grandchildren they are having extraordinary heavenly experiences. Why? Their lives aren't cluttered with the junk like adults are. They are pure in spirit and see God. I say they are extraordinary experiences however this is normal for them. They have no hidden agendas and aren't exaggerating.

*Blessed are the pure in heart, for they shall see God. (Matthew 5:8)*

One thing my granddaughter shared with me was about the playgrounds in heaven. She did not have understanding about what she was seeing yet it was very clear. She began by telling me about all the gold in heaven. Months earlier she saw gold angels and the golden streets. But now she's weeping as she began telling me about the silver-gold children playing on the gold playground. She said, "These are all children that were never born. Something happened to them while they were in their mommy's tummy and they weren't born. But they are in heaven with Jesus and having so much fun playing together!" I knew she had seen aborted babies as well as miscarried ones. I explained that sometimes something happens when a baby is inside the mommy's tummy and the baby can't be born but they go straight to heaven.

Children are innocent and pure in spirit. They are seeing and hearing clearly and adults need to be paying close attention to them. God has anointed this generation of children in a far greater way than any prior one. As custodial parents to this generation we had better pay attention because truths as well as warnings are coming through clean vessels. This is a chosen generation of children and I believe God is using them because many adults are too cluttered to hear clearly.

These little ones know how to hear God and when they pray they release a pure word that cuts out the twelve-step program. They go right to the root of the problem and people are healed or given a clear prophecy. We need to pay close attention to our children. They are pure in heart and speak with accuracy clear and simple straight from the heart of God.

## Mother Church
## Gains New Vision But Loses Control

This was an interesting dream because it involved my mother and my sister. In this dream my mother represented the church and my sister is Wisdom. As the dream unfolds, my mother is sitting in my living room. She's so excited because she just received new BIG RED GLASSES. I'm emphasizing them because they were huge. Also my sister got her a smoking patch.

My mother was really excited about this too because she had smoked for about seventy years.

I believe the church is not only getting better vision, she's going to see things through the blood of Jesus. She peers from a heavenly perspective not earthbound. It's like her eyes are going to be opened really wide. And the good news, the control spirit will be something of the past. Cigarette patches are used to control the urge to smoke and eventually quit altogether. I believe the church at large is going to transition into the holiness of God by laying down their control spirit. Then we will experience Isaiah 11:2 reigning supreme in the church.

*And the Spirit of the Lord shall rest upon Him—the Spirit of wisdom and understanding, the Spirit of counsel and might, the Spirit of knowledge and of the reverential and obedient fear of the Lord (**Isaiah 11:2 NKJV**)*

## God's Examining Table

I heard the Lord saying, "This is a season where secrets of our hearts are being revealed to all mankind whether good or bad. All mankind is on an examining table where God is inspecting them with His all-knowing eye. And there is no sin that will go unnoticed. There is absolutely nothing hidden from God. Either we fall onto the Rock or the Rock will fall on us."

*Jesus asked them, Have you never read in the Scriptures: The very Stone which the builders rejected and threw*

*away has become the Cornerstone; this is the Lord's doing, and it is marvelous in our eyes? I tell you, for this reason the kingdom of God will be taken away from you and given to a people who will produce the fruits of it. And whoever falls on this Stone will be broken to pieces, but he on whom It falls will be crushed to powder [and It will winnow him, scattering him like dust]. (Matthew 21:42-44)*

Over the years many things have been overlooked in the church for various reasons. But God is calling a spade a spade and it's time leaders begin confronting sin in the church. We can no longer turn our head and pretend we don't see it. We are well into the Laodicea church age but we do not need to remain there.

In Revelation 3 John records "I know your [record of] works *and* what you are doing; you are neither cold nor hot. Would that you were cold or hot! So, because you are lukewarm and neither cold nor hot, I will spew you out of My mouth! For you say, I am rich; I have prospered *and* grown wealthy, and I am in need of nothing; and you do not realize *and* understand that you are wretched, pitiable, poor, blind, and naked." **(Verse 15-17)** God was ready to spit them out of His mouth because of their hypocrisy. Yet He gave them another chance to make things right. **(Verse 18)** Because He loves His children He convicts them of their sin so they will repent and turn from their wicked ways. **(Verse 19)** Leadership is responsible for the sheep and if they allow them to continue in their sin, they are held responsible.

*18 Therefore I counsel you to purchase from Me gold refined and tested by fire, that you may be [truly] wealthy, and white clothes to clothe you and to keep the shame of your nudity from being seen, and salve to put on your eyes, that you may see.*

*19 Those whom I [dearly and tenderly] love, I tell their faults and convict and convince and reprove and chasten [I discipline and instruct them]. So be enthusiastic and in earnest and burning with zeal and repent [changing your mind and attitude].*

The good news is this; He's standing at the door of our heart today waiting for repentant hearts. It's a win-win situation. Unfortunately many in the church have been led astray by the world system and they come to church to hide. And they remain hidden in their sin because there's no conviction of sin being taught. The truth has been watered down so much and compromised to the point that it's only an ear tickling 45 minutes once a week. Unfortunately programs and meetings have replaced truth and true power in the church.

It's an open invitation and church leadership is called to a higher standard. We must be like our Lord and love what He loves and hate what He hates. He loves the sinner but hates the sin. Bob Jones would say that if you allow someone to continue in their sin you are condemning them to hell. It is our place to inform, enlighten and speak the truth in love. We can't make decisions for others but we must tell them the truth.

This is not geared to the church alone. Parents have the same responsibility. If our children are dabbling in such things as drugs, alcohol, pornography and witchcraft and the parents don't address it, they are doing them a great injustice. Parents are afraid of losing their children, afraid of them running away, etc. I would rather take that risk then see them lose their soul. We are all on God's examining table and secret sin won't be tolerated any longer. The things done in secret are now being exposed. So if you don't want your dirty laundry exposed for the whole world to see, don't participate in the sin! Repentance is key. Let's keep a clean slate for behold, He stands at the door of our heart and knocks.

*[20]Behold, I stand at the door and knock; if anyone hears and listens to and heeds My voice and opens the door, I will come in to him and will eat with him, and he [will eat] with Me.*

*[21] He who overcomes (is victorious), I will grant him to sit beside Me on My throne, as I Myself overcame (was victorious) and sat down beside My Father on His throne.*

# Chapter Six
# Resembling Joshua 1

## The Coming Shift

I became aware of the coming shift in the body of Christ some time ago. Around 2015 the church began going through a shaking, a wakeup call and a transition. This transition closely resembles the transition of leadership that happened in Joshua. The Jordan represents a place where we shed off the past, the old man and those things that deter us. We emerge on the other side as a new creation, baptized into the unshakable church inheriting the future and promises that God has for us. About a year and a half ago I believe the whole body entered into it.

*After the death of Moses the servant of the Lord, it came to pass that the Lord spoke to Joshua the son of Nun, Moses' assistant, saying: "Moses My servant is dead. Now therefore, arise, go over this Jordan, you and all this people, to the land which I am giving to them—the children of Israel.* ***(Joshua 1:1–2 NKJV)***

In the very first two verses of Joshua we see that there was a need to come to grips with the fact that Moses was dead, and so was the old way that kept them doing laps in the wilderness for 40 years. It was time for the Israelites to cross over. Much like them, the church has been in a holding pattern for a long time. Over the last year in general there has been a real shift in the body. People are being called to different locations. Some churches and ministries are being shaken in a way that disperses almost everyone. There can be a lot of circumstances, good and bad, for the shift but God is not surprised by any of it.

*"Wisdom calls aloud outside; She raises her voice in the open squares. She cries out in the chief concourses, At the openings of the gates in the city She speaks her words. (Proverbs 1:20-21 NKJV)*

No matter what the cause, God is catching people's attentions. Those whose attentions have been caught are being prepared for the crossing over that has been, is and will be taking place. As individuals, families, congregations and ministries, we are being shaken and need to come to grips with the fact that something has passed. That something is what prohibits us from entering into the unshakable promises of God. Even something that might have been great for us before is now of no benefit for the Kingdom of God and must be let go of before we can cross over.

## Promises, Parameters and Preperations

*Every place that the sole of your foot will tread upon I have given you, as I said to Moses. From the wilderness and this Lebanon as far as the great river, the River Euphrates, all the land of the Hittites, and to the Great Sea toward the going down of the sun, shall be your territory. No man shall be able to stand before you all the days of your life; as I was with Moses, so I will be with you. I will not leave you nor forsake you. (Joshua 1:3–5 NKJV)*

Verses 3, 4 and 5 involve the promises for Joshua. There is new territory in our unshakeable futures and it has both boundaries and privileges. Some would call the boundaries our "Sphere of Authority". For Joshua the boundaries were clearly laid out. Notice, though, it starts out saying "everywhere your foot shall tread" and then it defines where they shall tread. That is known as a place of effectiveness and protection.

The Israelites had defined physical boundaries laid out for them. We, on the other hand, are entering into something different. It is going to be different in every situation because every situation is different. There are places that are permissible but not necessarily profitable. Vice versa, there are places that we could go that are very profitable but not permissible. Some places are neither. Your "great sea" and "Hittites" might be completely different from another's. For what we're moving into it is vital that we find those parameters out.

*Be strong and of good courage, for to this people you shall divide as an inheritance the land which I swore to their fathers to give them. Only be strong and very courageous, that you may observe to do according to all the law which Moses My servant commanded you; do not turn from it to the right hand or to the left, that you may prosper wherever you go. This Book of the Law shall not depart from your mouth, but you shall meditate in it day and night, that you may observe to do according to all that is written in it. For*

*then you will make your way prosperous, and then you will have good success. Have I not commanded you? Be strong and of good courage; do not be afraid, nor be dismayed, for the Lord your God is with you wherever you go."*
**(Joshua 1:6-9 NKJV)**

Isn't it curious that the thought "Be strong and of good courage" appears 3 times within the 4 verses of 6 - 9. Joshua needed to be resolute. The first time it is in reference to "this people", the Israelites, and what he would do for them; dividing up for those who are in the Covenant. The second time gives a good layout of how to be strong and of good courage with the result of prosperity wherever you go. I feel that "Wherever you go" is a reference to those outside of the Covenant, the harvest if you will. The third time reminds me of Jesus calling us out of the boat like Peter. Peter's initial response is "If you call me to then I can do it". God says to Joshua and to us today, "Have I not commanded you". The transition is in full swing and it is a whole lot better to agree with God. Some struggle with thoughts like "Is that God's voice or not?" Step out of the boat towards where Jesus is calling you. Yes it is scary. Yes it is exciting. Yes there is great potential to mess up, but that stepping out is the place where we learn the most. To the voice of fear, anxiety, worry and doubt our response in this season is "Hasn't God commanded/called me? I'll be strong (in the Lord) and of good courage. I won't be afraid nor dismayed because the Lord my God is with me wherever I go.

*Then Joshua commanded the officers of the people, saying, "Pass through the camp and command the people, saying, 'Prepare provisions for yourselves, for within three days you will cross over this Jordan, to go in to possess the land which the LORD your God is giving you to possess.' " (Joshua 1:10-11 NKJV)*

I find it interesting that Joshua gets the Israelites ready with not much direction. I keep looking over these verses hoping to find more instructions. There's no mention of what to take, how long the trip will be or even how to pack. Pretty much it is "Pack up we're leaving in 3 days." God just didn't give the details out yet. Not only didn't God give the details out yet, but I want you to notice that Joshua didn't try to come up with a plan. That is where we are now. We have packed up whatever we felt we needed to follow God's call by faith because we don't know what is to come. We literally couldn't prepare for it because it is indescribable and if there were descriptions for it we would end up missing it like the Pharisees missed Jesus. Instead we have had the great opportunity to *"work out your own salvation with fear and trembling"*. In other words it is a time to draw in closely (Like John to Jesus' chest) to hear the still small voice and pack accordingly.

## Three Unlikely Tribes

*And to the Reubenites, the Gadites, and half the tribe of Manasseh Joshua spoke, saying, "Remember the word which Moses the servant of the LORD commanded you, saying, 'The LORD your God is giving you rest and is giving you this land.' Your wives, your little ones, and your livestock shall remain in the land which Moses gave you on this side of the Jordan. But you shall pass before your brethren armed, all your mighty men of valor, and help them, until the LORD has given your brethren rest, as He gave you, and they also have taken possession of the land which the LORD your God is giving them. Then you shall return to the land of your possession and enjoy it, which Moses the LORD's servant gave you on this side of the Jordan toward the sunrise." (Joshua 1:12-15 NKJV)*

Verses 12-15 revolve around the Reubenites, the Gadites, and half the tribe of Manasseh. These 3 tribes were given land outside of the Jordan's boundary before anyone even crossed the river. I understand some things from these verses but really I know that there is a lot more to be mined out than what I'm seeing. Those 3 tribes have special connotations with them. At first the Gadites made no sense to me, as to why they were in the group. Reuben was the first born to Jacob/Israel, and so the Reubenites made sense to represent the firstborn. Manasseh was the first born son of Joseph being a grandson to Jacob, and so the half tribe of Manasseh made sense as the firstborn of the next generation. But Gad was seventh in line; even if you look at the children of the bondservants he is the third. This made no sense. Why is Gad there?

Then He began showing me. Reuben is a child of Jacob and Leah. Leah represents two things. First being married to Jacob makes her a free woman. Secondly Leah represents the old nature, being in how she tricked Jacob into marrying her and also that the waiting time for her marriage was an easy instant thing.

With Rachel there was a long wait, or a high price up front and paid twice. Reuben therefore represents the free with the old nature.

Gad may have been born third in the order of the bondservants' sons but the first 2 sons were Rachel's. Gad is the first born son of Leah's bondservant. So this is what He showed me. Leah still represents the old man/old nature. Zilpah, Leah's bond servant, represents the slave. So Gad represents the slave in the old nature. This lines up because the free man (Reuben) is no better than the bond servant (Gad) in the old nature.

> *But we are all like an unclean thing, And all our righteousnesses are like filthy rags; We all fade as a leaf, And our iniquities, like the wind, Have taken us away.* **(Isaiah 64:6 NKJV)**

So now how does Manasseh fit in? Manasseh is the only tribe to occupy land on both sides of the Jordan and in this way has two different interpretations. From the east side of the Jordan, where Reuben's and Gad's lands were, the half tribe of Manasseh represents "half Hebrew and half Egyptian", or a mixture. Being Rachel's descendant, Manasseh can be seen as long-suffering, patient, costly and the Beloved. So the first interpretation, which corresponds with Reuben and Gad, is that Manasseh represents the Beloved who is still not fully purified. To look honestly at ourselves we are in that purification process.

So this all lines up; three different groups are going in. We have Reuben, those who know the Spirit and cling to their old nature.

We have Gad, those who know the Word and cling to their old nature. We have Manasseh, those who know the Spirit and Truth but are still processing out of their old nature.

All three tribes were given land ahead of the other tribes. Similarly today all three natures have received *"on earth as it is in heaven"*. As I mentioned earlier the whole body has entered in to the Jordan. All of the church is in some stage of the transition. All of us fall into one of those three categories. All three tribes were given the same charge which I will paraphrase, "leave all of your stuff behind and go ahead of those who haven't yet obtained and fight for them until they possess like you possess". That is both the same charge to us and part of the transition process. Jesus always says it best though.

*Then Jesus said to His disciples, "If anyone desires to come after Me, let him deny himself, and take up his cross, and follow Me. (Matthew 16:24 NKJV)*

Let me caution you not to disqualify any of the three types. Reuben, Gad and Manasseh entered into the Jordan coming from three different scenarios. I pointed out some of their lesser respectable interpretations, but they were still the ones called out from the others to go before the full company armed to assist and defend those who had not yet possessed. Were they called in their perfection or because of it, NO. *"There is none righteous, no, not one"* *(Romans 3:10)* Yet I'm reminded of what Bob would say. **"We are all perfect while being perfected".** You see God, Who called us into the Jordan, is calling from across the Jordan into His perspective which looks at us through Christ, our Perfection.

## What To Expect

After crossing the Jordan there are a few things that we can expect to see. **The first thing we can expect is a more concise platform.** At this point the whole body of Christ is baptized. Whether you've been transitioning for the last 5 years or just 5 days, we are all in the Jordan, so to speak. By being in the transition we are in, I can say that we are all standing on dry ground. The things that could have gotten us stuck and bogged down have all been dried up. Along with that, there are things we thought we could count on that just aren't there. It isn't a bad thing; we are right where we are supposed to be. If we packed too much stuff for our journey ahead don't worry, it'll be left in the Jordan. That is what the Jordan is there for: to get rid of the things that won't be beneficial on the other side.

**The second thing we can expect is a coming out on the other side.** Now I can't guarantee how much longer that the shaking, transition, birthing, baptism, crossing over will take, but I can say that the light on the other side has begun to appear. Some of the body will begin emerging in 2020 and some will remain in transition for a while. So hang in there; agree with God quickly, let go of what you need to because the other side is almost ready for us to come out on.

**The third thing we can expect is a oneness on multiple levels.** I mentioned that Manasseh represents two different interpretations. The first one was left on the east side of the Jordan. Manasseh on the west side, Promised Land, represents a completely different nature and a very wonderful plan. That different nature can be seen as Christ. As Jacob prophetically crossed over Manasseh to pass the blessing onto Ephraim, so did God the Father pass over Jesus to bless us.

*For whom He foreknew, He also predestined to be conformed to the image of His Son, that He might be the firstborn among many brethren.* **(Romans 8:29 NKJV)**

Manasseh was Joseph's firstborn. Joseph was Rachel's firstborn and Rachel was Jacob's beloved. So Manasseh is not only a picture of Jesus but he also represents God's Beloved and the next emerging generation or the new man, those "foreknown and predestined to be conformed to the image of His Son". It is a perfect picture of being one with Christ, but that is only the nature. There is also the plan.

We saw three tribes entering into the Jordan ahead of the others, but there was only one of the three that ended up possessing inside the Promised Land. Here is the plan. Through this transition we're going to see only one new creation come out. It's going to be one new man emerging from where the three old men were laid to rest in the Jordan. So we can really expect to see ourselves becoming one with Christ on many levels.

**The fourth thing we can expect is that things have been spied out for what you've been called to.** Remember Joshua said *"for within three days you will cross over this Jordan".* Guess what happened during that three day period. The spies were sent out ahead of the crossing. **(Joshua 2:1-24)** When our feet are coming out on the other side we're going to start getting reports, updates, strategies, Godly Wisdom and counsel to accomplish our calls: helping others possess as we have possessed.

**The fifth thing we can expect is leadership to claim new possession in the Promised Land. (Joshua 4:1-18)** Those stones pulled from the Jordan were much more than a memorial to the successful crossing. These stones were also boundary markers, laying claim to the 'promised land' of Canaan by the people of Yahweh. I saw them set, not lying down, but as pillars. Pillars have two ends. One end touches Heaven and one end touches Earth. I see new leadership emerging and either working with or replacing existing leadership.

**The sixth thing we can expect is Unprecedented Salvations.** Manasseh again represents the new, emerging and next generation in Christ. Yes we are coming out of the Jordan as a new creation, but the calling remains the same: help others possess as we have possessed. If we have all come through in possession of the promise, who then are we helping? There remains then a great harvest for us to fight for and assist.

**The seventh thing we can expect is a sign of the new level of faith.** In Joshua 5:1-12 Joshua circumcised all the Israelites who had not been circumcised during their time in the desert, and they celebrated the Passover festival at Gilgal. Now the previous generation had all died in the desert except for Joshua and Caleb. That means everyone received that mark. Likewise there will be a circumcision for the emerging generation. There will be a noticeable difference in those that have come through this transition. This mark will apply to both the Manasseh's and Manasseh's harvest.

And he received the sign of circumcision, a seal of the righteousness of the faith which he had while still uncircumcised, that he might be the father of all those who believe, though they are uncircumcised, that righteousness might be imputed to them also. **(Romans 4:11 NKJV)**

# Chapter Seven
# Two Current Seasons and a Physical Manifestation of Binoculars

## Season of Shaking What Can Be Shaken

The main season that we are in, which I touched on in chapter 6 is a Season of Shaking. One main reason that we are continuing through this season of shaking is to develop our discernment. It has been going on for a few years for us now. It has been pretty rough too. Many who go into a season of shaking don't necessarily understand why they are in it or what it is for. Most of us, when the shaking starts, go into a preservation mode. The shaking begins revealing what things we hold most important; potentially what we hold more importantly than God. When the shaking starts, where do we run? When the shaking starts getting rough what are we holding on to? Not everything that we embrace is necessarily wrong, but the purpose of the shaking is for us to let go of the things that are holding us back from embracing Him. It is there to assist us in our transition from who we are into who He has called us to be.

*See that you do not refuse Him who speaks. For if they did not escape who refused Him who spoke on earth, much more shall we not escape if we turn away from Him who speaks from heaven, whose voice then shook the earth; but now He has promised, saying, "Yet once more I shake not only the earth, but also heaven." Now this, "Yet once more," indicates the removal of those things that are being shaken, as of things that are made, that the things which cannot be shaken may remain. Therefore, since we are receiving a kingdom which cannot be shaken, let us have grace, by which we may serve God acceptably with reverence and godly fear. For our God is a consuming fire. (Hebrews 12:25–29)*

Notice that even the heavenly things that can be shaken will be shaken. Yes some of those things need to be removed because they're holding us back. There is a coming shift even in the atmosphere; that new creation is readying to emerge. I would start practicing to let go of anything because the shaking that we've been experiencing is going to increase. Firstly, as I mentioned, it is for us to move into who we are called to be. Secondly it is going to increase and the world is really going to start feeling it. The shaking is coming on those in the world for the same reasons that it has been coming on us; to make us all not of the world, to move us all into a more secure foothold in the Lord. The eventual goal for all is to fully receive that kingdom that cannot be shaken.

*And behold, I am coming quickly, and My reward is with Me, to give to every one according to his work. (Revelation 22:12)*

*For the time has come for judgment to begin at the house of God; and if it begins with us first, what will be the end of those who do not obey the gospel of God? (1 Peter 4:17)*

Not every time, but a lot of times when I see or hear the word "judgement" I find it interchangeable with the word "reward", and vice versa. This shaking comes first upon the church so the church can come through unshakable and presented to the world that is in desperate need of salvation. As the Church we just get to choose to partake first of the same promise that the world gets presented with a little later.

The scribes who were tasked with copying the scriptures by hand, pre-printing press days, would baptize themselves before each time they referenced God. You may ask "Why bring this up?" Because similarly God is baptizing all; leading with Christ the Head, then secondly the Church or the Body, and then those who have the opportunity to choose to join in with the Body. All are baptized into one body. Historically we look back and say that those baptisms were revivals or moves of God. They are all one and the same.

Naaman, in 1 Kings 5, dipped seven times to rid himself of his leprosy as Elisha had instructed. Like Naaman, we, as the Bride, have been going through baptisms continuously throughout history. Each time the body of Christ dips in that Jordan, the baptism takes something of the fallen world off of us. Each time we go through that process a new creation emerges cleaner and closer to God. The shaking partly gets us into the Jordan, but then it intensifies in the Jordan to encourage us to let go of the stuff that keeps us from taking hold of the promises waiting for us.

# Season of Where Did We First Meet?

One season that we are in and will continue to be in is a returning to the place where we first encountered Jesus, Holy Spirit and/or Father God. During this time not only the first meeting places, but in those places where we have significantly met with God, there will be significant discoveries and resources to be found. These discoveries and resources will not only deepen our original perspectives but they will also enrich and equip us in and through our current situations and help propel us more accurately into His heart for our calling. During this time those who retrace even their salvation experiences will find rejuvenation, hidden manna, heavenly strategies and even new depths to the truths that they first started walking in.

This is actually a very strategic part that we can all participate in. In Joshua 4 the leaders of each tribe were called upon to each take a large stone out of the Jordan that they just crossed and place each stone in the place that they would camp at that night. They were referred to as memorial stones, but they were more than that. In a trance I saw them set up like pillars. They were not piled up like rocks; nor were they randomly placed around. They were strategically set up as boundary markers and as territorial claims. In Joshua's time these stones were claims on the physical Promised Land for the Israelites.

In this Season of "Where Did We First Meet?" we are coming up out of our Jordans and are called to take possession and assist others in taking possession of the Promises of God. The Jordan experience is the place where we all first met God. We went in knowing that He was calling us and that there was a salvation on the other side. We thought we left everything behind when we entered in, but that season of shaking got more intense in the dry crossing and we began letting go of things that were unnecessary in obtaining the promises on the other side. But even as some may have already come out on the other side they are being called back in their first meeting places for those stones. Those boundary markers are treasures that God placed in our first meeting places that we can carry out of current Jordan experience and use as our claims in the promises of God.

There is a difference in standing on a large rock in a dry river bed and carrying a large rock out of a dry river bed. These truths, promises or revelations that we've stood on in the past are as ready as they are going to get to be carried out. They are going to be weighty. It is going to take a lot, and in some cases everything, to get these claims to our camps before it starts getting dark. But these Rocks are for those who are soon coming. They need to be in place before the shaking really comes.

These boundary markers need to be set like pillars. A pillar has two ends to it. One end touches Heaven while the other touches Earth. We need to get these truths, promises and revelations lined up on Earth as it is in Heaven, not partially but absolutely completely and unwaveringly. Those coming across after us are going to need these claims and boundary markers in place.

# Binoculars On My Toaster

One morning as I was getting breakfast ready for the family I noticed a pair of binoculars sitting on my toaster oven. They were not there the night before. In fact they never were there before because we didn't own a pair of binoculars. I checked the house for any signs of a break in and discovered that there had not been one. We called around to some people who had been over to our house within the last few days and, not surprisingly to us, no one had left a pair of binoculars on our toaster. Spiritually everything felt safe, so I began asking the Lord what this meant and why they were there? Here is what I've gotten.

## 1. Agreeing With The Word Brings Things Far Off Closer (Binoculars on the Toaster)

There is hope in the Word of God. It is a revelation of His love for us and among other things His plan(s) for us. Many times though there is a long period between the promise and the reception. The first thing I would like to point out is our agreement with His promises. Among some of the things that God has planned for me is for me to lead worship from behind a bass guitar. I have struggled with this plan for years. Finally I am agreeing with it. I started speaking the agreement a few years ago and building my faith towards it. That spoken agreement began bringing something that to me seemed impossibly far off, a lot closer.

I began seeing more invitations to move into God's plans as I started agreeing with them. We'll say that vocally agreeing with God's promises is like picking up a pair of binoculars and looking through them. It begins to give you a clearer closer picture. In actuality it moves you closer towards that promise. Of course the opposite is true too. If we speak against the promises of God then it moves us further off. So this is a time of bridling our tongues into agreement. That vocal agreement eventually needs more than words though; which brings us to….

## 2. Testing The Word (Bread in the Toaster)

I'm going to liken Testing the Word/Promise of God to placing our bread into the toaster. It is an act of trust in the Word of God. That vision/promise that we are agreeing with needs to be tested. We need to start practicing those promises. For me I can agree with God all I want about leading worship from behind a bass; if I don't practice then I don't gain experience. Without testing out the promises I have no idea what works and what doesn't. Someone called to be an evangelist needs to start agreeing and then get out there and find out what all that entails for them. What are the boundaries of this promise; what does God want to do through it, etc. I began voicing my agreement with God's plan and then asked Him for opportunities. The doors opened within a week. He wants us to agree with Him and succeed. So it is a time for those who have vocally agreed to begin practicing their promises.

## 3. Toasting The Word (Heat Is Applied)

It is AWESOME to start moving, on assignment, in the promises of God! These assignments, however, are not permanent landing places. In comparison with eternity our lifetimes are vapors in the wind. When we come into agreeing with God's promises here on earth, no matter how long it may be, it is a temporary assignment. In these temp jobs there is always a testing going on. Heat is always being applied somewhere. It should at least be comforting then that they are only temporary assignments.

Heat is always being used on the Word received. It draws out the character in the individual with the Word. It can burn off the dross and be used to purify. 1 Corinthians 3:12-13 refers to the fire testing each person's work on Judgement Day, however each of our remaining days on assignment we have fiery testing that we can use to check our characters and line them up if they are out of biblical spec.

*Now if anyone builds on this foundation with gold, silver, precious stones, wood, hay, straw, each one's work will become clear; for the Day will declare it, because it will be revealed by fire; and the fire will test each one's work, of what sort it is. (1 Corinthians 3:12-13)*

That heat also changes the state of things that we carry within us. It will either burn something up or make it bubble up. We are essentially like teapots having received the Word in our lives we get set on the burner. Then the heat is applied. Eventually what was tepid inside of us heats up and gets excited. But the teapot stays on the heat. Eventually the heat takes care of any threats from within but the teapot stays on. It keeps getting hotter until what is bubbling inside of it begins pushing air out.

Still it stays on the heat. It has to hit the right pitch before it comes off.

We are the same way. That word in us needs the heat applied to it so it can get us purified. The promise starts bubbling inside and the heat goes up a notch. Some things that are out of line get exposed and the heat goes up again. We submit everything to God and the heat goes up some more. The promise really starts bubbling out now. We start speaking about the promise but maybe without conviction. We stay on the heat a little longer and maybe the next opportunity we are surer of that promise, and so we speak with more anticipation. We stay on the heat until our hearts are speaking in total agreement with the promise of God. When we hit that pitch of agreement we are ready to pour out.

## 4. The Word Extending Our Vision (Toaster and Binoculars Working in Conjunction)

I see the Word having been agreed with, tested and toasted to then nourish others and give them a hope. It will be a lifeline to some, a lighthouse to others and a grappling spot to even others. In any case you will have a warm fresh Word from God and it will extend the vision of others to see past their situations and enable them to be able to see into God's heart for them. Not only that but they will be able to do something about it. This in turn will nourish us and extend our vision.

# 5. Two Visions Through One Heated Word

That heated Word is going to cause some changes too. It is going to take people from being hearers of the Word to being Doers. We are going to see an increase in people's faith as they hear our testimonies of the Word fulfilled. That faith will continue to increase until they begin to manifest that Word.

*And they overcame him by the blood of the Lamb and by the word of their testimony, and they did not love their lives to the death. (Revelation 12:11)*

The "Blood of the Lamb" is what God has done for us, His provision for our situation. The "Word of our testimony" is how we've individually applied the "blood of the Lamb" to our lives. Speaking another's testimony has a bit of power in it but really if that hasn't been applied personally it isn't doing you any good. Once it is personally applied you are working with power. The greatest overcoming power comes in setting your life aside for what God is doing.

So let's look at the whole thing. It starts with a revelation of God. Maybe a truth or strategy is imparted to us. We begin agreeing with it until it is time to test it. We go out and try it out; we figure out how it applies best in our lives. At this point we move from moving in faith into ministering. Along with that ministering comes heat from every direction. The character of Christ gets developed into us through the heat that comes after the promise. We reach a pitch of agreement with God and it is then time to pour out. This is a whole different level because it is now replicating in others to where they move from hearing to agreeing, from agreeing to speaking, from speaking to ministering and so on.

*How then shall they call on Him in whom they have not believed? And how shall they believe in Him of whom they have not heard? And how shall they hear without a preacher? And how shall they preach unless they are sent? As it is written: "How beautiful are the feet of those who preach the gospel of peace, Who bring glad tidings of good things!"* **(Romans 10:14-15)**

## 6. Who Is The Toaster

*till we all come to the unity of the faith and of the knowledge of the Son of God, to a perfect man, to the measure of the stature of the fullness of Christ* **(Ephesians 4:13)**

That is the end goal. Revelations, prophecies, teachings, words of knowledge and such are for us for now. They are for bringing us all to the measure of the stature of the fullness of Christ. When that is accomplished there will then be no need for them. The end goal is best said "on earth as it is in Heaven". Knowing Him and then making Him known will continue for us until knowledge is done away with.

# Chapter Eight
# Three Confirming Dreams

## Dream #1
## Theft-Proof Currency and Leo the Lion

The dream started with my wife Katie and I in a financial institution. We owed some money and it was time for our payment. Katie was given a new type of currency. The coin was a rounded square shape. It was gold colored and about an inch thick. They said that it was a $2 nickel. We had a couple different coins given to us. They told us that it was a new theft proof currency. I jokingly said that no one would think to steal it because it did not look like currency. It seemed that we could only fit one in our pocket at a time, but it fit nicely. Katie was also given five $100 quarters. We handed one of our quarters in as a payment.

The dream now changed as I left the bank area and walked out through the front door of the house I grew up in. Katie stayed in the doorway. I walked down our front steps and out to the middle of the street. There from the street I looked back towards Katie and noticed a lion standing where we used to store our fireplace wood on the first landing at the top of the hill. He was very broad. I was not afraid of him but I could see his back. The area of skin covering his spine opened up. From somewhere around his shoulders or his head came a pair of antlers. They rotated around from a swiveling point around his shoulders until they were facing with points forward. Instantly I remembered having seen him before in another dream. The other dream also involved him with antlers but he also had a unicorn horn and a row of spikes along either side of his spine. In the other dream I know that there were other creatures like the lion but I can't remember them as of yet. This however was the end of my dream.

## Interpretation #1

I believe that there are new levels of protection coming over our finances. The enemy is going to find it more difficult to steal provisions from God's children. All of those coins were squares, meaning the theft-proof currency is a value system being set up within the Body of Christ with each line upon line having been set at a right angle. But the edges were rounded meaning those values have been tested over a long period of time and have been found to be of great value. I think that the Lion is another level of the new security. Value is going to be placed in some unlikely areas that appear to have little or no value. It is a key time to invest wisely with God in unlikely places. In some cases I am speaking of finances, but it can be kindness, encouraging words or time and energy. Those small amounts of investments will bring much larger returns. Think of it; two dollars returned on a nickel and one hundred dollars returned on a quarter. What do you think the return would be if we went all in?

I think in the second part of the dream that the lion-creature represents Leo the constellation. After doing a bit of research I found that there is a star, in the constellation Leo, where the neck meets the shoulders named "Algiebor". "Algiebor" means "the head", but connecting from it there are some more stars to the top of it known as "the sickle", which if you look at it looks like antlers going forward. Algiebor is also the beginning of the back of Leo and is actually made up of 2 stars that apperar to be 1 star because they are so close together from our perspective. It reminds me of the 2 rows of spikes on either side of the spine. I think it at least signifies a time for investing and/or harvesting in the next few months.

It was a very broad lion, about 1 ½ times or so broader than any picture that I've seen and it stood up at a higher level. This security has a broader coverage than before. It is not a street-level security but has a higher vantage point. Anything coming against God's provision is going to have a high level heavenly lion to deal with. Those antlers coming out from his shoulders are a level of protection rooted from a place of authority. So I think it would be a good time to make sure that we are lined up on the side of the provisions of God.

## Dream #2
## The Counselor, the Gi and Going Through Customs

Part One of the dream started with Katie and I at a counseling session. The Counselor had just finished up our session and it was time to pay. We were being charged as two different people. Katie's amount was around $120. My amount was more, around $280. We both went to hand the Counselor our checks. The Counselor told me that my session had already been paid for. In fact someone had already paid for all of my sessions. I was not sure who had prepaid for me but I handed the Counselor my check anyways and said to put it towards Katie. I looked to see how much had been prepaid towards my account. It was hundreds of dollars over $7000.

As I was wondering who had paid for my counseling session the Counselor added that something else was bought for me as well. It was an older looking two piece black Karate outfit (Gi). At the bottom of the Uwagi (jacket) there was writing that went all the way around. The golden lettering was in a heavenly language. Although the outfit was very neatly folded, I could see everything. There were a couple of things that I noticed that were woven into the Gi. Two things specifically had been sewn in, a piece of a ballistic weapon (like a gun trigger), and a piece of technology (resembling a RAM chip). They were not originally part of the Gi. They had been added in for now. The Counselor explained a little bit of that and also said that the Gi was being sent across the border with a couple things added into it. The pieces being added were parts of larger devices that would instantly be flagged at customs if they went across as the larger devices. Going through customs as a small insignificant piece would not raise suspicion. This was being done all over.

The Counselor then spoke specifically about the Gi. He said that it was very old and of the highest quality. I cannot express correctly what it was likened to. Seeing that it was very similar to a karate gi, I felt that it had been like a Japanese Emperor's. Anyways, the counselor said that when anyone who knew anything about gis would see this Gi that they would instantly recognize the greatness of it. Part One faded out.

Part Two transitioned to sometime after I had crossed through customs. I was now wearing the Gi. Katie and I were seated at what I guess was the drop off place. I do not exactly remember seeing the piece of the gun or the piece of technology in this part of the dream but I knew that we were handing them off at some point. Katie did not really interact but she was there. There were two men in the room with us sitting on the opposite side. If I had not seen the Counselor in the first part of the dream I would have discounted them as being shady characters. They began explaining about the pieces coming through customs. They had a way that they kept track of everything. All of the different pieces, what they went together with to assemble things, who had what and where they were all had been kept track of.

A person, who I believe was an angel, came in to hand off an item to the two men. After a brief interaction between them it was my turn. I believe one of the two men saw the writing on my Gi while I was still seated. He instantly recognized it and fell down on his knees and began worshiping. I was really not sure what to do with that. I put my hands on him to pray for him. That's when I woke up.

## Interpretation #2

There seemed to be a lot of Heaven and Earth references hidden in the representations of twos. First it was a two-part dream; The first part in the counselors room which I believe is heaven, and the second part in the handoff room which I believe is earth. The second reference to heaven and earth is Katie and I. As a couple the husband represents the Lord who is in Heaven, the bride represents the Earthly manifestation of the Church. The third reference to Heaven and Earth is in the Gi itself. The Gi is a two piece martial arts uniform. The Uwagi is the upper jacket part that in my dream was written on in golden unreadable glyphs and I believe represents Heaven. The Shitabaki is the lower pants part of the uniform that I believe represents Earth. We are in a defined season where we have things lining up on Earth as it is in Heaven. Some of that is preordained and we are just there as it happens, but some of it is based on our decisions and responses. Someone paid for all of my session and gifted me a priceless ancient outfit. None of that was my doing, but I chose to receive them.

Holy Spirit is the Counselor and Jesus paid for my sessions and the Gi. The Gi itself I think is my mantle, but I believe there are many other mantles being handed out at this time. Before I go on with interpreting I want to be clear on something. Your mantle is wrapped up in your calling, gifting, character and nature among some other things. A lot of people want someone else's mantle because it has already been revealed. All of the hard work has been done. *Love endures long and is patient and kind; love never is envious nor boils over with jealousy, is not boastful or vainglorious, does not display itself haughtily.* **(1 Corinthians 13:4)** Our own mantle is the only mantle we should be after. It is what Jesus offers to each of us and it is uniquely custom fit for our callings. It was all black which symbolizes the

Bride. I was told it was very old although it didn't look worn or faded.

Interestingly enough I had this dream the morning that the Emperor of Japan abdicated the throne. His successor's name means "A man Who Will Acquire Heavenly Virtues". I think this is not a word for just me but for the Body. There are mantles available. They have your Heavenly Virtues, your calling, your nature, your character and your giftings in them. It probably doesn't look like mine or any other. It is yours and it is time for you to receive it and walk in it. There are things in your mantle that are uniquely you and it will lead you and cover you in ways that another's wouldn't.

There are also things woven into your mantle for this time. This is a confirmation with "Resembling Joshua 1". That shaking season has been used to move people to new locations and to mix things up. We could look at it as cross-pollination. In that though, we are carrying things within us, that we might not even be aware of, that will be combined with others in the new locations. God is keeping track and has things set up. If we went to a new location with the whole plan of God it would get stopped on the way there. We are all getting shifted around and getting set up for the next phase. All the pieces will start coming together after we come up out of the Jordan.

The 2 items sewn into the Gi have special meanings. The gun triggers are our triggers in God. On a gun you could say that every piece is the most important piece. The trigger however sets everything in motion. Without it there is no life to the gun.

Without it there is little to no threat to the enemy. I think we are getting ready to start really firing at the enemy in the next little while. Intercessors are going to see what a trigger can do in their battles.

The RAM chip deals with our memories. R=Random A=Access M=Memory. God is going to start making sense of our memories that seem like random events. They are going to start lining up so that we can see God revealed through the events. All of the ups and downs and events that were rough places are going to be evened out so that you can see the Lord's hand with you through it all.

> *The voice of one crying in the wilderness: "Prepare the way of the LORD; Make straight in the desert a highway for our God. Every valley shall be exalted and every mountain and hill brought low; the crooked places shall be made straight and the rough places smooth; the glory of the LORD shall be revealed, and all flesh shall see it together; for the mouth of the LORD has spoken." (Isaiah 40:3-5)*

A hard drive represents storage space or where all the information is kept. RAM represents the amount of workable space for that information. Some of us will be rebooted in ways to wipe away things that are clogging their workable space and in essence free them up. Some will be expanding their workable space. It can be for being able to get things done are for taking on additional tasks. I would caution you though on what else you agree to take on. There is a temptation that comes with that freedom that can clog you right back up. Use a little wisdom, say "no" to some things, and you will actually get more done.

# Dream #3
# Facing Fear

In the beginning it was a little fuzzy but I became aware of large sections of land being rearranged. They were from the size of small neighborhoods up to the size of half of a small town. They were sliding around like those picture puzzles that have one square missing.

I began to focus in on a section of land and started noticing some of the wildlife there; in particular there was a full-grown lion chasing a very large deer. The deer was probably a little smaller than a moose. It had one antler coming out of the top middle of its head. The antler arched up and forward directly. It had five points on it and all five points pointed forward. From the side it was angled resembling those old tin openers. The deer was actually much larger than the lion but that didn't seem to be taken into account.

The lion seemed like a very normal lion and looked like it was chasing the deer for fun or sport. When it finally caught the deer it opened its mouth and swallowed the deer whole. It re-minded me of the seven emaciated cows swallowing the seven fat cows whole. **(Genesis 41)** The lion made no slashing swipes at the deer. It did not bite the deer. After about 10 seconds it opened its mouth and the deer ran out. The lion repeated this about four or five times.

After about the fifth time something different happened. The lion had each time swallowed the deer from the tail end. The deer must have gotten tired of this because it turned around and faced the lion. The deer then walked towards the lion, not charging, but not backing down. The lion opened its mouth again to swallow the deer. The deer just walked into the lion's mouth. I thought to myself "this was the smartest thing that the deer could have done". Going in facing the lion would allow the deer to use its horns and really do some damage to the interior of the lion.

My focus changed now to notice that I was about 50 foot or so away from that scene. I was wondering if I was too close to what was going on when I noticed directly in front of me a black jaguar ready to swipe at me. He came up really close to me and I batted it away with my right hand. It came at me again and I batted it away with my left hand. The third time I batted it away with my right hand. The fourth time I batted it away with my left hand. The fifth time I finished it with my right hand. Then I woke up.

## Interpretation #3

I think this is just more confirmation of the transition that we are all going through; except that it was on a large scale that I could see. I don't think that it is happening to only the Church, but whole areas.

The deer represents the Church, ministries, individuals, etc that have been running from something for a long time. They've been swallowed up and spat out by the same thing multiple times as they have been fleeing for their safety. But we have been given something to combat our adversities with. Like that deer's antler it is part of our heavenly nature.

I find it interesting that the antler was singular and in the middle of the deer's head. It wasn't one antler that had remained after a fight. It was the only one that had ever grown on the deer's head, like a unicorn. I think that the shape of the antler resembling a tin opener is important. We can face that fear now, go right into the midst of it and take care of it once and for all.

*Therefore humble yourselves under the mighty hand of God, that He may exalt you in due time, casting all your care upon Him, for He cares for you. Be sober, be vigilant; because your adversary the devil walks about like a roaring lion, seeking whom he may devour. Resist him, steadfast in the faith, knowing that the same sufferings are experienced by your brotherhood in the world. But may the God of all grace, who called us to His eternal glory by Christ Jesus, after you have suffered a while, perfect, establish, strengthen, and settle you. (1 Peter 5:6-10 NKJV)*

That lion had no claws or teeth, just like the adversary not having any power over us except for what lies we believe. If we turn and run away adversity chases us and swallows us, but it can't hold us. We can flee from adversity when we come out of it or face it. Like Shadrach, Meshach and Abednego said *"If that is the case, our God whom we serve is able to deliver us from the burning fiery furnace, and He will deliver us from your hand, O king. But if not, let it be known to you, O king, that we do not serve your gods, nor will we worship the gold image which you have set up." (Daniel 3:17–18 NKJV)*

Bob Jones had a list of 10 types of cats that represented adversities that faced people. The least on this list was a house cat ranking as 1 and the greatest was a lion ranking as 10. I'm not sure if a jaguar was on the list, but I'm glad that I deflected all of its attacks and sent it away. The lion being at the top though means that it is going to be one of our biggest fears that we have the opportunity to take down.

# Summary

The year of the mouth is the breath of God – His glory!

Out of God's breath the worlds were created. He said, "Let it be!" And everything was created in its fullness, its mature state containing seed bearing ability to reproduce of its own kind. After God created, He rested. Therefore from that place of rest we can speak to our mountains and they MUST move. They have no choice because we are speaking on His authority.

No longer are we striving with God because we've entered into His rest. His Sabbath rest is one of the promises of "yes and amen." In Bob Jones' 100 year prophecy the Lord revealed to him that the body of Christ would move from having the faith of God (2010-2019) into having the rest of God (2020-2029). Therefore in this time where the body of Christ is transitioning from seeing (Ayin) to speaking (Pey), it is also transitioning from faith to the Sabbath rest of God.

Individually the body of believers is crossing their personal Jordan River according to the level of their commitment to Christ. (Ezekiel 47:1-12) Some will go deeper and therefore higher while others may take longer to get to the other side. Regardless the remnant is moving and following the arc of His glory. I'm saying arc not ark (as in the ark of His covenant). Recently the Lord showed me that there's coming an arc and the wave is so high no man can withstand it. This arc and wave are so tremendous and powerful the only way to survive is to fall on your face and worship God.

2020 is the year of the mouth! The Lord has been revealing to me many different points regarding the words we speak and how we use our mouth. It's time to open wide your mouth and let God fill it. **(Psalm 81:10b)** There's no need to be timid or shy, just allow the Lord to speak through you. Just remember that Satan is the prince of the power of the air **(Ephesians 2:1-3)** so Christians need to get their words in alignment with the Father. Jesus spoke only what He heard His Father saying. **(John 12:49)** In the same way we must follow His example. If not we hand our authority over to the evil prince of this world's system. And we remain as sons of disobedience **(Verse 2)** agreeing with the "lusts" of the world **(Verse 3)** instead of the "gifts and fruits" of the Spirit. We eat the fruit of our words and reap their harvest. Life and death are in the power of the tongue **(Proverbs 18:21)** as well as blessings and cursing. Let's speak life according to the will of God and His kingdom.

*And you He made alive, who were dead in trespasses and sins, in which you once walked according to the course of this world, according to the prince of the power of the air, the spirit who now works in the sons of disobedience, among whom also we all once conducted ourselves in the lusts of our flesh, fulfilling the desires of the flesh and of the mind, and were by nature children of wrath, just as the others. (Ephesians 2:1-3)*

Watch as the glory of the Lord rests upon His remnant. And the words they speak will be full of power and authority. Get ready for miracles in the midst as the remnant proclaim from the secret place of the Most High. Watch as evangelists take to the street to bring in the harvest of souls. Pay special attention to young children as they prophecy the new day on the horizon. What they see in heaven they shall proclaim on earth and it shall be done according to the fullness of His Glorious Majesty. Amen.

# About the Authors

Bonnie Jones is passionate about the love of the Lord and bringing that understanding to the body of Christ. Her desire is to see the body move in unity and learn to love unconditionally. She encourages the body to hear the voice of God for them and obey what they hear. She's strong on the "spoken word" and believes that "you live with the consequences of the choices you make, so choose wisely!" Bonnie's a real stickler for truth and therefore carries a strong mantle of justice. She has a great love for children of all ages and speaks into their destinies. She is also a strong advocate for women to move into their rightful place in the body of Christ in power and humility.

Bonnie continues to walk in the same type of anointing as her late husband Bob Jones did and carries on his mandate to ask the body "Did you learn to love?" She has written several books including The Shepherd's Rod from 2008-2019, The Eagle, 341, Fruit of the Spirit and her personal favorite The Power of the Spoken Word.

For information regarding scheduling Bonnie Jones to speak at your next event or conference, please contact her at bonnie@bobjones.org.

Lyn Kost graduated from MorningStar University with an Associate's Degree in Christian Ministry and from Lifeway College in New Zealand with a Bachelor's Degree in Graphic Art and 3-D Animation. As Administrator for  "Bob and Bonnie Jones Ministries" since 2008, he manages multiple websites, designs, records, documents, edits and produces all products for the ministry.

Like the prophet Nathan, Lyn delivers accurate words through the gift of faith. His love for the Truth is evident as he moves in the gift of inspired prophetic teaching and as he ministers the gospel throughout the world. As the Lord has directed him, Lyn currently leads worship and assists from behind a bass guitar at "Abundant Hope Church" in Pineville, NC. His greatest joy is his wife Kathryn and their children Olivia, Avalyn, Sophia and Ephraim.

Lyn Kost has worked on layout and design for The Shepherd's Rods from 2009-2019, The Eagle, 341, Fruit of the Spirit, The Power of the Spoken Word and Did You Learn To Love?. He has co-written the 2014 - 2019 Shepherd's Rods and is working on a few other books to be announced in the near future.

For information regarding scheduling Lyn Kost for speaking, worship, book and/or ebook formatting and design work please contact lyn@bobjones.org.

# Available Products

Visit our "didyoulearntolove.org" website for a complete catalog of our resources including a variety of books as well as other products and capture Bob Jones' teaching cd's and dvd's.

## 2019 Shepherd's Rod

## 2018 Shepherd's Rod

## 341

## Fruit of the Spirit

## The Eagle

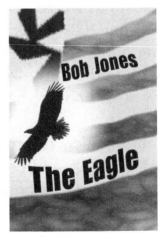

## 2017 Shepherd's Rod

## 2016 Shepherd's Rod

## Did You Learn to Love?

## Power of the Spoken Word

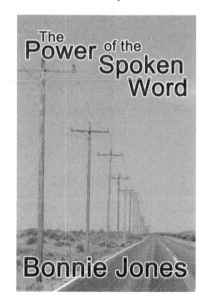

## "Did You Learn to Love" products include:

Cups
Travel Mugs
Tote Bags
Journals
T-Shirts
Wristbands
Pens

Made in the USA
Monee, IL
12 February 2020

21677835R00075